# monarchy

## REBECCA STEFOFF

**Marshall Cavendish**
Benchmark
New York

Marshall Cavendish Benchmark • 99 White Plains Road • Tarrytown, NY 10591
www.marshallcavendish.us

Library of Congress Cataloging-in-Publication Data Stefoff, Rebecca, 1951- Monarchy / by Rebecca Stefoff. p. cm. — (Political systems of the world) Summary: "Discusses monarchies as a political system, and details the history of monarchies throughout the world"—Provided by publisher. Includes bibliographical references and index. • ISBN-13: 978-0-7614-2630-1 1.Monarchy—Juvenileliterature.2.Monarchy—History—Juvenile literature. I. Title. II. Series. JC375.S76 • 2007 321'.6—dc22 2006026384
Photo research by Connie Gardner Monarchy credits Cover photo by Bettmann/CORBIS Photographs in this book are used by permission and through the courtesy of: *Corbis:* Bettmann, 1, 3, 5, 61; Gianni Dagli Orti, 15, 25, 69; Bojan Breceij, 27; Alinari Archives, 45; Burstein Collection, 48; Archivo Icongrafico, S.A., 66, 77, 80, 110-111; Royal Palace, 104; Jack Dabaghian/Reuters, 101; *Getty Images:* Hulton Archives, 8, 91; *The Image Works:* Spectrum Colour Library/ Heritage Images, 12; The British Library/ Tohpham, 52; Mary Evans Picture Library, 74; Hu Weibiao/Panorama, 97; *The Granger Collection:* 18, 38, 63, 83, 85.
Publisher: Michelle Bisson • Art Director: Anahid Hamparian • Series Designer: Sonia Chaghatzbanian • Printed in Malaysia
135642

WITH THANKS TO PROFESSOR TOM DANDELET OF THE DEPARTMENT OF HISTORY AT THE UNIVERSITY OF CALIFORNIA AT BERKELEY, FOR HIS EXPERT REVIEW OF THIS MANUSCRIPT.

# Contents

monarchy

# The King Is Dead! Long Live the Queen! ▮ ▮ ▮

**1**

CLOUDS HUNG OVER LONDON on the afternoon of Tuesday, June 2, 1953. Rain fell in spatters. The brightest thing in England's capital city was a golden coach that passed slowly through streets lined with three million people. Some of those people had camped on the sidewalks since the evening before. They wanted to be sure of having a clear view of the coach—and perhaps, if they were lucky, a glimpse of the person inside it.

The coach drew to a stop in front of the historic church known as Westminster Abbey. A dark-haired young woman named Elizabeth stepped out of the coach and entered the high-ceilinged Abbey Church of St. Peter, Westminster. On either side of the center aisle, the church was crammed with guests. Among the eight thousand people present were prime ministers, presidents, and princes from around the world.

Elizabeth reached a small square stage called the theater, built especially for that day's events. She sat on a chair and faced the audience. A solemn hush filled the Abbey, broken only by the faint whir of television and movie cameras. Forward stepped the Archbishop of Canterbury, the highest-ranking clergyman of the Church of England, the country's state religion. Turning toward the east, he spoke these words:

"Sirs, I here present unto you Queen Elizabeth, your undoubted Queen. Wherefore, all ye who are come this day to do your homage

9

**Queen Elizabeth II was transported to her coronation in a golden carriage that looked like it had escaped from *Cinderella,* but which was, in fact, the real deal.**

and service, are ye willing to do the same?" A choir of schoolboys cried, "God Save Queen Elizabeth!" and trumpets blared in response.

The archbishop repeated his question to the north, the west, and the south. The trumpeters and boys repeated their responses. The ritual known as the Rite of Recognition was complete. The Rite of Recognition, however, was just the beginning of a much longer ceremony: a coronation. By the end of the ceremony, the twenty-five-year-old Elizabeth would wear a crown that symbolized her position as monarch of the United Kingdom of Britain and Ireland and all its dominions.

## "A SENSE OF HISTORY"

Elizabeth did not become queen on her coronation day—she had already been queen for more than a year. Her father, King George VI, died in his sleep in February of 1952, leaving two daughters as heirs to his throne. Elizabeth, the elder daughter, was first in the line of succession. In a process called accession, she proclaimed herself monarch and was recognized as queen by the government. At that time she stated, "By the sudden death of my dear father I am called upon to assume the duties and responsibilities of sovereignty. My heart is too full for me to say more to you today than I shall always work, as my father did throughout his reign, to advance the happiness and prosperity of my peoples, spread as they are all the world over."

The coronation ceremony that took place sixteen months later was merely the final step in the process of confirming Elizabeth's claim to be the legitimate successor to the throne. It was also a public performance that celebrated not just the young queen herself but also the long history of monarchy in England and throughout Europe. Above all, the coronation ceremony was layered with tradition. Every ritual and symbol, every gesture and garment, awoke echoes of the past. The coronation of Queen Elizabeth II, one of the major monarchic events of the twentieth century, summed up a thousand years of royal history, legend, and myth.

After the Rite of Recognition, attendants brought forward and placed on the altar a set of precious and very valuable objects. One was Saint Edward's Crown, named for Edward the Confessor, who was king of England from 1042 to 1066. The crown had been made in 1661 to replace an older one that had been destroyed. Also placed reverently on the altar were a second crown; a golden rod called the royal scepter, topped by the 516.5-carat Star of Africa diamond; a golden, bejeweled ball called the sovereign's orb; an ivory rod that ended in a carved dove; a royal ring set with sapphires and rubies; and a pair of spurs, a sheathed sword, and a set of bracelets. These items were pieces of England's regalia—its national collection of crown jewels and royal symbols.

The archbishop then administered the royal oath to the queen. He began: "Will you solemnly promise and swear to govern the peoples of the United Kingdom and Northern Ireland, Canada, Australia, New Zealand and the Union of South Africa, Pakistan and Ceylon, and all of your Possessions and other territories to any of them belonging and pertaining, according to their respective laws and customs?" The wording of this part of the oath reveals the central feature of the British monarchy: It is a government in which the monarch cannot rule by whim, or according to his or her own desires, but must follow the law of the land.

"I solemnly promise so to do," Elizabeth replied.

"Will you," the archbishop continued, "to the uttermost of your power, cause Law and Justice, in Mercy, to be executed in all your judgments?"

Elizabeth answered, "I will."

In the next and final part of the oath, the queen pledged to uphold the Church of England, or the Anglican church, as it is sometimes called. This pledge reflects the tangled history of church and state in Great Britain. In the early years of the sixteenth century King Henry VIII established the Church of England with himself as its head, largely because the Roman Catholic Church would not grant him a divorce. Ever since that time, the ruling king or queen of England has been both the head of state and the official head of the national church.

After Elizabeth had sworn and signed the oath, the archbishop presided over a religious service. Then, in preparation for the next phase of the ceremony, the queen moved to a different chair—Edward's Chair, also called the Coronation Seat. It was built on the order of another early king of England, Edward I, who reigned from 1272 to 1307. The Coronation Seat is not a splendid throne of jewel-encrusted gold. Instead it is a wooden chair of no great size, supported by four legs shaped like lions. Experts think that the chair was once handsomely painted, perhaps even decorated with gold leaf, but today it is simply

The Oath of Allegiance Throne bears Queen Elizabeth II's initials. This is the chair on which the queen sat for her coronation in 1953.

old oak, marked in places by the carved graffiti of bygone centuries. Since 1308, every reigning English monarch but one has sat in this chair to be crowned. But the Coronation Seat's importance in English history and legend has much to do with what rested *under* the seat for all those coronations.

Edward I had the chair built especially to hold a precious piece of plunder called the Stone of Scone. This slab of rock came from Scotland, where the early Scottish kings used to sit or stand on it for their own coronations. The Stone became a symbol of Scottish pride, power, and destiny. Then, in 1296, Edward I stole it and carried it off to London to lend its symbolic power to English coronations. The Stone fit neatly into a compartment directly under the seat of the chair Edward had built for it, and there it remained, despite many demands from the Scots for its return—claims that echoed their demands for independence from English rule. So prized was this chunk of sandstone that on Christmas Day 1950, two years before Elizabeth was crowned, some Scottish students hid in Westminster Abbey, sneaked away by night with the Stone of Scone (it broke in two pieces as they removed it), and carried it back to Scotland. Pressure from the British government, however, led Scotland to return the Stone in time for Elizabeth's coronation. (In 1996, seven centuries after Edward I took the Stone of Scone from Scotland, the British government formally returned it to Scotland—on the condition that England could borrow it for all future coronations.)

Once Elizabeth had taken her place on the Coronation Seat, she was ready for an ancient part of the ceremony called the anointing. While four knights held a golden cloth above the queen's head, the archbishop raised a golden spoon and a small golden container known as the ampulla. He poured a few drops of oil from the ampulla into the spoon and then dripped them onto Elizabeth's head and hands, saying, "And as Solomon was anointed king by Zadok the priest and Nathan the prophet, so be you anointed, blessed and consecrated Queen over the peoples whom the Lord your God has given you to rule and govern."

The words spoken during the anointing refer to an event described in the Old Testament of the Bible, when Solomon became king of the ancient Israelites. According to tradition, kings received the right to rule from God, speaking through priests and prophets who blessed the ruler with sacred oil as a symbol of divine favor. The anointing of Queen Elizabeth, however, had roots in history as well as in religion.

The ritual recalls a turbulent era of king-making and competition among the nations of Europe.

It started in France sometime around the year 506. Clovis, a pagan chieftain of the Frankish tribe, had become king. He married a Christian woman who was determined to convert him to her faith. Finally Clovis swore that if the Christian God granted him victory in a coming battle, he would allow himself to be baptized as a Christian. Clovis won the battle and kept his promise, but when the time came for his baptism in the cathedral in Rheims, France, the bishop discovered that he had no holy oil with which to anoint the king. At that time in history, anointing was a standard part of the rite of baptism. It had also taken place at coronations in many pagan, Jewish, and Christian lands. The events at Clovis's baptism, however, turned anointing into an issue of national policy.

According to French legend, a dove flew into the Rheims cathedral carrying in its beak a small vial of oil straight from heaven. The bishop anointed Clovis with the oil, and afterward the holy vial became one of France's great treasures. By the ninth century, no king could be recognized as the true ruler of France until he had been anointed at Rheims with oil from the vial, which somehow managed to refill itself between anointings.

The French took great pride in this gift from God, claiming that their holy oil was better than the oil used to anoint the kings of other countries (the non-French anointing fluid was usually olive oil that had been blessed by a priest or bishop). Tired of such boasts, the English produced a miracle of their own. They said that the Virgin Mary had given a vial of holy oil to Thomas Becket, an archbishop of Canterbury in the twelfth century who was later made a saint. The English claimed that their oil was even holier than the French oil, and they began using its container, called the ampulla, in their coronation ceremonies.

Modern scholars have shown that the story of Clovis, the dove, and the vial from heaven dates from the ninth century. An archbishop of Rheims named Hincmar invented it, possibly to boost the status of his cathedral or of the French monarchy. The origins of the English ampulla are equally worldly. Still, the ampulla has become a treasured piece of English regalia, and the ritual of anointing remains an important part of the coronation ceremony. It is a moment in which the ruler is seen not just as the head of a political state but also as a link between the earthly and divine realms.

After Queen Elizabeth II had been anointed, her coronation continued. Court officials presented her with the spurs and the sword; she accepted them and returned them to the altar. The archbishop took the bracelets from the altar and fastened them onto the queen's wrists, saying, "Receive the bracelets of sincerity and wisdom, symbols and pledges of that bond which unites you with your peoples." These bracelets, called armillae or armils, are reminders of the earliest days of medieval kingship when Germanic tribal chieftains wore armbands as signs of their rank.

Other officials stepped forward to drape a royal robe and a royal stole over Elizabeth's shoulders and to hand her the golden orb. They placed the sapphire-and-ruby ring on her right hand and gave her the sceptre and the ivory rod, symbols of royal might and mercy, to hold. Finally the moment of actual coronation arrived. The archbishop placed Saint Edward's Crown on Elizabeth's head and spoke words that had been uttered at English coronations since the eleventh century: "Stand firm and hold fast from henceforth the Seat and State of Royal and Imperial Dignity which is this day delivered unto you, in the name and by the authority of Almighty God and by the hands of us the Bishops and servants of God, though unworthy."

Every nobleman and noblewoman of Britain who was present in Westminster Abbey that day then put on his or her own coronet, or small crown. A great shout of "God Save the Queen!" echoed through the church, trumpets sounded, and a signal from the roof of the Abbey set off a booming salute from the cannons at the Tower of London, some distance away.

The final phase of the ceremony was the homage, when the newly crowned queen's subjects knelt before her and vowed to be loyal. First was the archbishop. Then came the young queen's husband, who saluted the queen with the words, "I, Philip, Duke of Edinburgh, become your liege man of life and limb and of earthly worship." Next, representatives of each rank of the British aristocracy paid homage, kneeling before Elizabeth and kissing her right hand, to the accompaniment of anthems, drums, trumpets, and shouts of "Long live Queen Elizabeth!"

With the homage completed, Elizabeth removed Saint Edward's Crown and donned the Imperial Crown, which was made in 1838 for the coronation of Queen Victoria. The Imperial Crown contains within itself a vast sweep of English history. Among its gems are a huge ruby said to have been worn in battle by King Henry V, pearl earrings that belonged to the first Queen Elizabeth, a sapphire from King Charles II's crown, another sapphire from the ring of King Edward the Confessor, and a 309-carat gem cut from the Cullinan Diamond, found in South Africa. The Imperial Crown is considered the most valuable crown in the world. It is an instantly recognizable emblem of monarchic majesty.

Wearing this crown, with the jewelled orb and scepter in her hands and the royal robe trailing behind her, Queen Elizabeth walked out of Westminster Abbey and through a wildly cheering crowd. She climbed into the golden coronation coach, which began the journey back to Buckingham Palace, the royal residence in London. This journey through the city streets was much more than a carriage ride. It was a royal progress, a ceremonial public passage that reinforced the bond between the people and their sovereign. Like the coronation ceremony itself, the progress was part of a long tradition. Its purpose was to remind people of their heritage, to link the present with the past—and it fulfilled that purpose. "Those who attended the coronation . . . or who watched it on television and the cinema," wrote British social historian Harold Nicolson in his 1962 book *Monarchy*, "were above all else impressed by a sense of history."

## QUESTIONING THE MERITS OF MONARCHY

Nearly every monarchy known to historians has had its royal symbols, as well as rituals to accompany them. Not all royal symbols are bejewelled objects of great value, like the British regalia, but all of them serve an important purpose: connecting a new ruler with the history and traditions of the past.

The ritualized, symbol-laden coronation of Queen Elizabeth II was steeped in tradition, but it was also very modern in one important way—media exposure. The British Broadcasting Corporation (BBC) made elaborate arrangements to broadcast the entire event live on radio and television. Although a film of the coronation was later shown in movie theaters around the world, it was the television broadcast that truly marked the modern marriage of monarchy and the media.

The coronation show was the most ambitious television and far-reaching production up to that point in BBC history. Broadcast in forty-four languages and viewed by about twenty million people around the world, it ushered in the age of televised royal events as mass entertainment. In 1953, television was still relatively new to many people. Not all households had sets. Throughout the United Kingdom and its far-flung dominions, in Australia and Canada, and many other places around the world, sitting-rooms filled up as people crowded around their neighbors' sets to watch the queen receive her crown. Those who couldn't squeeze into the rooms clustered outside, watching through windows. Street parties formed wherever the owner of a television set placed it on a front step. News reports the next day were full of accounts of people weeping and fainting, overcome by their emotions as they viewed the spectacle.

Those tears and swoons were evidence that something about the British monarchy triggered strong emotional reactions in viewers. On one level, monarchy is an impersonal institution, a system of government. On another level, monarchy is embodied in the people who have reigned as kings and queens, emperors and empresses, over the centuries. Either way, monarchy has long aroused powerful passions—not all of them favorable.

One of the best-known and most influential attacks on monarchy was the pamphlet *Common Sense*, published in 1776 by Thomas Paine, who had emigrated from England to the North American colonies little more than a year before. George Washington and many others credited *Common Sense* with helping to inspire the colonies' Revolutionary War for independence from Great Britain and its king, George III. Paine began by arguing that human beings in a simple, natural state live happily without a government. When they come together in larger societies for mutual help and comfort, however, they need some form of government—but even the best government is a necessary evil.

Paine then outlined the faults of the British system of government, a monarchy with a constitution. According to Paine, the British people, in trying to preserve their ancient monarchy while adopting some of the principles of a constitutional republic, had created an illogical and absurd government. Their belief that this system was a good one, Paine declared, came "as much or more from national pride than reason."

The government and king of Britain were not Paine's only targets.

# COMMON SENSE;

ADDRESSED TO THE

# INHABITANTS

O F

# A M E R I C A,

On the following interesting

# S U B J E C T S.

I. Of the Origin and Design of Government in general, with concise Remarks on the English Constitution.

II. Of Monarchy and Hereditary Succession.

III. Thoughts on the present State of American Affairs.

IV. Of the present Ability of America, with some miscellaneous Reflections.

---

Man knows no Master save creating HEAVEN,
Or those whom choice and common good ordain.
THOMSON.

---

PHILADELPHIA;

Printed, and Sold, by R. BELL, in Third-Street.

MDCCLXXVI.

In 1776, Thomas Paine wrote *Common Sense*, a pamphlet that shook the world. Many credit Paine's writings with inspiring the birth of independent democracy in America.

He also aimed his powerful, emotional arguments at the institution of monarchy itself. He questioned the idea that one individual was destined to rule over many. The distinction between kings and their subjects, Paine said, was purely artificial. He asked how the great mass of people had come to believe that kings were a different order of being, superior to ordinary folk, and why people let kings dominate them. "Male and female are the distinctions of nature," he wrote, "good and bad the distinctions of heaven; but how a race of men came into the world so exalted above the rest, and distinguished like some new species, is worth enquiring into, and whether they are the means of happiness or of misery to mankind."

Monarchy was bad, but hereditary succession—the practice by which a throne passed from a king to his offspring—was even worse. "To the evil of monarchy," wrote Paine, "we have added that of hereditary succession; and as the first is a degradation and lessening of ourselves, so the second, claimed as a matter of right, is an insult and an imposition upon posterity." By this, Paine meant that submitting to a monarch's authority diminishes a person's dignity, but letting the monarch pass that authority on to generations of offspring was an insult to the dignity of one's own children, who would be expected to submit to those future monarchs.

Paine thought that it was highly unlikely that the same family would produce two or three or more rulers in a row who were equally virtuous or competent. Even a good king's children or grandchildren could prove inferior to him. But had any kings ever *been* good? Paine suspected that if he could strip away the centuries and view the origins of the great royal houses of Europe, he would "find the first of them nothing better than the principal ruffian of some restless gang, whose savage manners . . . obtained him the title of chief among plunderers." Finally, Paine concluded that "[t]he nearer any government approaches to a republic the less business there is for a king" and that a single honest man was more valuable to society than "all the crowned ruffians that ever lived."

Thomas Paine's fiery antimonarchism played a part in the rebellion that turned Britain's American colonies into the independent republic known as the United States. After that revolution, Paine spent years trying to persuade the people of Great Britain to abolish their monarchy and establish a true republic. He failed, for the simple reason that most people in Great Britain in the late eighteenth and early nineteenth centuries believed that monarchy was the proper form of government. But that was two centuries ago. What about today?

In 2000, a poll of a thousand British adults revealed that 63 percent of them favored Great Britain remaining a monarchy, and 67 percent of them felt that the monarchy had an important role to play in Britain's future. According to the same poll, however, only 35 percent believed that the monarchy would still exist in 2050, while only 20 percent felt that it would survive to 2100.

Another poll taken two years later may have forecast the future of the British monarchy. Among the overall British population, the percentage that favored keeping the monarchy had risen to 74 percent, possibly because of excitement caused by the recent Golden Jubilee, the celebration of Queen Elizabeth's fifty years on the throne. But among Britons who were between fifteen and twenty-five years old, only 54 percent—a slim majority—wanted Britain to remain a monarchy. As those younger Britons grow up, support for the monarchy may wane. In fact, it may already be waning. A 2004 poll showed that if Queen Elizabeth II were to abdicate, only 47 percent of people would favor keeping the monarchy unchanged. Thirty-seven percent called for a scaled-down monarchy, with fewer members and fewer responsibilities. Seventeen percent preferred replacing the monarchy with an elected head of state, while 2 percent chose none of those three options.

What is the nature of monarchy? Does it help or harm a nation? These questions are not new. Philosophers, political thinkers, and ordinary citizens have asked them again and again throughout history. Today they are being asked not just by Britons but by people in dozens of countries around the world, from Andorra to the United Arab Emirates, that have some kind of monarchical government. These modern monarchies have inherited a form of government that may be the most ancient of all—but one that is still evolving.

# 2

## Monarchy and Its Origins

WHAT IS MONARCHY? In simplest terms, it is a government with a monarch, a man or woman who is the sole head of state and holds office for life. Often, but not always, monarchy is hereditary, passing from one generation to the next in the same family; unlike dictators, monarchs are usually considered to have been born into the job. Whether called king, queen, emperor, empress, prince, or princess, a monarch differs from other heads of state, such as prime ministers and presidents, by being regarded as a sovereign, someone who embodies in his or her person the identity of a country or realm, as well as control over it.

Originally, a monarch had supreme authority and was truly the ruler of the land. Today, however, few monarchs enjoy undivided authority. Now the term *monarchy* generally refers to a state that has a royal family and a hereditary head of state. But in many such states, the monarch's role in rulership has been reduced, the country operates under a constitution, and the real work of governing is done by a parliament, legislature, council, or similar group. This body may be headed by a prime minister, premier, or president whose office is more powerful than the monarchy. In such cases, the monarch is said to be the head of state, while the prime minister or other political leader is called the head of government.

Since the eighteenth century, many new governments have taken shape around the world. There have been republics and dictatorships, states based on the economic theories of socialism and communism, and nations governed by religion. Very few new monarchies, however, have been created. Instead, in many parts of the world, old monarchies have died out or been violently overthrown. Yet although monarchy's fortunes have waned, it remains alive. It is one of the oldest known forms of government, with roots deep in prehistory.

## PRIEST-KINGS AND PHARAOHS

Monarchy originated long before the beginning of written history, and it developed independently in many parts of the world. The majority of cultures have myths, legends, and folklore about ancient kings. Often these legendary rulers are said to have founded their civilizations through some heroic or mythical act, such as vanquishing a terrible foe or bringing the gifts of the gods to the people.

Moving from prehistory to history, some of the oldest written texts found by archaeologists tell of monarchic societies that were already old when those texts were written thousands of years ago. By studying these ancient texts, as well as oral and written accounts of kingdoms that developed more recently, scholars have formed a picture of how the earliest monarchies probably emerged.

Before there were monarchs there were tribal chieftains, community leaders, and heads of clans or large family groups. As societies grew larger and more complex, these leadership positions became more structured and formal. At some point, a leader was no longer a paramount chieftain or the matriarch of a clan: he or she was a king or queen.

Any one of a number of factors could raise someone to leadership, depending upon the group and its circumstances. Success in battle, the support of a majority of the group, skill in speechmaking or in settling disputes, wisdom, wealth—these made individuals stand out from the crowd. One factor, though, was vital. A leader had to be connected to the beliefs of the people. Victory in war could make someone a leader, force or threats could keep him in power, but for the concept of monarchy to survive, rulers had to fill a deeply felt need. Most often, that need was spiritual or religious. As historian W. M. Spellman points out in *Monarchies: 1000–2000,* "In virtually every society where monarchy emerged and flourished, this transformation was effected by anchoring the institution of royal authority in a deeply religious culture."

In the ancient world, leaders were thought to link earthly society to a higher order of magical or religious belief, just as they do today in traditional, unmodernized societies. By taking part in sacred rituals, and also by ensuring that society was properly ordered, rulers caused the gifts of the gods to flow down to earth. This meant, for example, that rain fell when needed, and crops were abundant.

At the same time, the rulers communicated with the gods on behalf of society. They asked the gods for help or advice to benefit the people. In some cultures, the monarch was also the tribal shaman, high priest, or chief religious leader. In other cultures, the religious leaders were separate from the monarchs, but the monarchs needed the approval or blessing of those religious leaders to reign. And in still other cultures, the monarchs came to be seen as more than priests or communications channels to the gods. They became representatives or descendants of the deities. Some monarchs even considered themselves to be gods, and so did their subjects.

The civilizations of the ancient Middle East are the oldest ones from which written records survive. According to those records, kingship was closely bound up with religion in the early states of Mesopotamia (now Iraq and parts of Syria and Turkey) and nearby regions. In some states, the ruler—almost always male—had the title *sanga*, which was the same word used for the chief official of a temple. In others, the king was described as "beloved of god" or "named by god." In all ancient Mesopotamian societies, rulers performed in religious rituals that were thought to be essential to a society's survival, such as offering food to the deities and participating in fertility rites (usually by ceremonially marrying a priestess who represented a goddess). Underlying the institution of royal rule was the universal belief that monarchs were chosen or favored by the deities. If enough people believed that a king had departed from the will of the gods—if, perhaps, droughts or military defeats made them think that the gods' favor had been withdrawn—they could rebel, overthrow the king, and select a new monarch.

North of Mesopotamia was the land of Khatti, in the central part of what is now Turkey. Its people, called the Hittites, became a formidable power in the ancient Middle East. The nature of the relationship between religion and royalty in the Hittite kingdom is clear in the words of a ritual in which a priest blessed the king: "May [the king] be dear to the gods! The land belongs to the storm-god alone. Heaven, earth, and the people belong to the storm-god alone. He has made [the king] his administrator and given him the entire Land of Khatti. [The king] shall continue to administer with his hand the entire land. May the storm-god destroy whoever should approach the person of [the king] and the borders of Khatti!" To the Hittites, the king was under the god's protection and functioned as an overseer of the god's territory,

The Akkadian dynasty, or royal family, ruled most of Mesopotamia from about 2350 to 2193 BCE. The Akkadian rulers took the blend of royal and religious elements a step further. One of the kings, Naram-Sin, claimed that he actually *was* a god. A surviving inscription says that the people of his city asked the gods to send one of their number to rule over them, and they got Naram-Sin. Yet Naram-Sin was also the grandson of a powerful earlier king, Sargon, who had fused many conquered city-states into the empire that Naram-Sin inherited. Historians speculate that Naram-Sin may have taken on the persona of a god so that he could claim superiority over the lesser kings whose cities he ruled.

In the early Middle Eastern monarchies, the approval of both the gods and the people established a king's rule as legitimate, or rightful. Monarchs were seen as servants of their states, at least to some degree. But by the time the kingdom of Babylonia rose in southern Mesopotamia around 1500 BCE, the power of kings had grown. Monarchs were now the outright owners of their territory. They could do with it as they pleased, such as trade it to another monarch as part of a marriage agreement or peace treaty, without concern for the will of the people. By this time, various classes of kings were recognized. The Great Kings (some of whom could be considered emperors) ruled large and powerful states such as Egypt, Babylon, and Assyria. Smaller nations or states that had been conquered or absorbed by those realms still had kings of their own, but those lesser kings acknowledged the overlordship of the Great Kings.

Monarchy appeared among the ancient people of Israel around 1000 BCE. According to the Bible, before the Israelites had kings they were governed by judges who interpreted law and religion. When the

This bronze sculpture dated circa 2250 BCE depicts the head of either Naram-Sin or Sargon, Akkadian kings who ruled most of Mesopotamia for about 150 years.

judge Samuel grew old, he appointed his sons to take his place, but they "did not follow his ways; they wanted money, taking bribes and perverting justice." The people said to Samuel, "So give us a king to rule over us, like the other nations." When Samuel prayed for guidance, God told him, "Obey the voice of the people in all that they say to you, for it is not you they have rejected; they have rejected me from ruling over them. . . . Well, then, obey their voice; only, you must warn them solemnly and instruct them in the rights of the king who is to reign over them." Samuel warned the people that a king could abuse his rights and oppress them, but still the people demanded a king who would be their leader and fight their battles. Samuel appointed a man named Saul to the kingship, and the Israelite monarchy was founded. David succeeded Saul as king, and Solomon succeeded David. In varying forms and through a number of dynasties, the monarchy lasted for several centuries.

The biblical account of how monarchy came to Israel was written centuries after the events it claims to describe. Most scholars regard it as a story that describes a profound shift in Israelite political organization. From a society of loosely linked tribes, the Israelites became a more centralized state under royal rule, with all the strengths and weaknesses of monarchy.

The ancient Israelite or Hebrew kingdom had features of both elective and hereditary monarchy. The first king was chosen, but in later years kingship generally passed from father to son. Always, though, a king required the approval of the priests, who were believed to speak for God. The idea that a king's right to rule came from God later had great influence on the idea of monarchy as it developed in Europe. The anointing of Queen Elizabeth II at her coronation in London was a symbolic link to the God-given kingship of the biblical monarchs.

Nowhere in the ancient Middle East was kingship more closely tied to religion than in Egypt. The Egyptian kings, called pharaohs, had many responsibilities. As supreme rulers, they made all decisions for the country in war and peace, although they generally consulted with advisors and turned much of the decision making over to underlings. As heads of the justice system, they were expected to administer the law with wisdom and fairness. And as chief high priests of the land, they presided over religious rituals intended to keep the relations between humans and gods in good order.

The Egyptian pharaohs were both religious and political rulers. This fresco is of a pharaoh wearing a crown ornamented with a cobra.

The pharaohs were so closely identified with the divine realm of the gods that modern scholars used to think that the Egyptian kings had actually been worshipped as living gods. Many leading Egyptologists now think that the nature of ancient Egyptian kingship was more complex than that. The pharaohs were indeed believed to become divine beings upon their deaths, when they ascended into the sky and merged with the sun god. During their lives, however, the pharaohs were not always considered to be living gods. Rather, they were originally seen as the human holders of an office that had been created and maintained by the gods. The monarchy itself was divine; the monarchs were simply the chosen instruments of the gods. Yet over time the notion of a special connection with the gods became ever more closely associated with the royal bloodline. The pharaohs came to be regarded as semidivine, related to the gods. One result was that intermarriages often occurred among members of the pharaonic families—cousin and cousin, uncle and niece, or brother and sister— because the pharaohs wanted their children to inherit the semidivine bloodline from both parents. The Incas of South America and a few other groups practiced royal intermarriage for the same reason: to maintain the purity of a bloodline that was not just monarchic but divine.

## GREEK IDEAS ABOUT KINGSHIP

The earliest known writings on political theory come from the ancient Greeks, who laid the foundations for many branches of philosophy and science. The Greeks observed the world around them, asked questions and pondered possible answers, and, above all, arranged knowledge and ideas into orderly categories and frameworks. Among other things, they described and classified political systems. But the Greeks did more than observe and write about political systems—they also experimented with them. Over time, the various Greek states had many different types of government, including monarchy, dictatorship, and an early form of democracy. Greek thinkers' comments on these and other forms of government were the first attempt to create a political science, and they have influenced other political thinkers for more than two thousand years.

The Greek states originally were monarchies with kings who ruled in the ancient style of tribal kingship. This type of monarchy is sometimes called Mycenaean after Mycenae, a powerful kingdom in southern Greece. It is also called Homeric kingship because it is illustrated in two epics about the Mycenaean era, *The Iliad* and *The Odyssey*, which have been linked to an ancient poet known as Homer. In the Mycenaean or Homeric version of kingship, the monarch was above all a war chieftain, capable of heroic battle feats and military leadership. Mycenaean monarchy was both hereditary and based on merit. Kings inherited their thrones, but they were expected to be worthy of them, or risk being cast out of power.

By about 800 BCE, most of the Greek monarchies had collapsed, overthrown by aristocrats who challenged the rule of kings. These elites were originally the military leaders of communities. When the aristocrats overthrew monarchies and took control of the state, they became civic leaders. They created a form of government the Greeks called oligarchy, or rule by a few. In time the definition of aristocracy broadened beyond the military elite to include the wealthy and socially prominent members of society. Aristocracy became hereditary in most places. Aristocrats were born into their elite social class, although an ordinary man could enter the oligarchic class through wealth or high achievements.

Some Greek states retained the aristocratic oligarchy for centuries. In others, soldiers rejected the aristocrats and put leaders of their own choosing in charge. These new leaders, called tyrants, were unlike monarchs because they came to power through force or the threat of force, not through heredity or the approval of the elites. The rule of tyrants was essentially dictatorship.

As tyranny became a common form of government throughout Greece, some tyrants proved to be better rulers than others. A few were capable and unselfish leaders. In the end, though, people usually overthrew the tyrants. When this happened, a few states returned to oligarchic government by the aristocrats. More often, however, citizens began to wield power through assemblies that made decisions, settled disputes, and elected officials. By allowing a large number of citizens to participate in these assemblies, the Greek city-states were moving toward some degree of democratic government. Historians of government often single out Athens, in particular, as the birthplace of democracy—even though a large number of Athenians, including women and slaves, were kept from having political power, and even though the Greek political philosophers feared pure democracy, which they saw as rule by an undisciplined, uneducated mob.

The Athenian philosopher Socrates (around 470–399 BCE) tried to define good and just government. The local authorities, regarding Socrates as disruptive and potentially subversive, had him put to death. Socrates's student Plato, however, recorded and expanded on Socrates's ideas in a series of dialogues, which are discussions of philosophical topics in the form of written conversations. The dialogue known as *The Republic* contains the kernel of Plato's political philosophy and describes his vision of a ruler he called a philosopher-king.

*The Republic* is a conversation in which Plato gives Socrates's description of the ideal political organization. In such a state, power would be wielded by a group of wise and just rulers called guardians, who would be trained in philosophy. They would lead austere, simple lives, untroubled by such cares as family life and private property, and they would guide the community so that all would be orderly and productive. Socrates freely admits, however, that such an ideal is probably impossible to achieve in the flawed world of human beings. The best that can be hoped for among human societies is a special kind of monarchy.

By the time of Socrates and Plato, the Greeks in general had a low opinion of monarchy, partly because they had fought a long series of destructive wars with the Persian Empire, which was an absolute monarchy. Proud of their own governments, which they considered more advanced than those of the Persians, the Greeks tended to regard monarchy as despotism in which the king's subjects were little more than slaves (although slavery existed in all Greek states). Still, the Greeks knew that monarchy was a very common form of government, and they drew distinctions between bad monarchies and better ones.

The best possible monarchy, according to Socrates (as related by Plato in *The Republic*), is one in which either kings become philosophers (seekers of truth and wisdom), or philosophers become kings. Socrates even outlines the proper education for a philosopher-king: After studying five kinds of mathematics, he would study philosophy to the age of thirty-five. He would then have fifteen years of practical experience in the world, such as by holding military office. Those who completed this training could, at the age of fifty, devote the rest of their lives to philosophy—specifically, to the study of what is good, and how to order their own lives and the community according to what is good. They would, however, serve as rulers when it was their turn to do so, and they would help educate those who would rule after them.

After outlining these imaginary good governments, Socrates then describes several kinds of bad governments that create unjust states. One bad form of government is democracy, in which individuals are confused by the notion of "freedom" and give way to all of their desires, not knowing what they really want. The worst kind of government, though, is tyranny, when a state is ruled by an all-powerful individual who answers only to his own passions, not to law or the community.

Plato's student, Aristotle (384–322 BCE), became one of Greece's most influential philosophers. The author of works on many branches of science and philosophy, he wrote about monarchy and other systems of government in *Politics*. While *The Republic* consisted largely of abstract speculation, *Politics* can be read, at least in part, as a practical guide for rulers. Aristotle explains the origins of the Greek states and other politically organized societies by saying that humans are by nature political beings who want to live together, and that they require some form of organization in order to do so. He uses the term constitution to refer to the way each society distributes power, or the right to govern. Whether a constitution is good or bad depends upon whether it benefits society as a whole (good) or only the rulers (bad). Aristotle writes that "constitutions which aim at the common advantage are correct and just . . . while those which aim only at the advantage of the rulers are deviant and unjust, because they involve despotic rule which is inappropriate for a community of free persons."

Another way of categorizing governments was whether power was wielded by one person, by a few people, or by many people. Each of these three possibilities had a bad form and a good form. The bad form of rule by one person was tyranny. The good form was monarchy. The bad form of rule by a few people was oligarchy—domination by a small group, usually the rich, without regard to their qualifications for leadership. The good form was aristocracy, or rule by the best, an elite group of citizens from good families, with good educations and high ideals. Turning to rule by the many, Aristotle declared that the bad form was democracy, which spread power among the poor and ignorant. The good form was what Aristotle called polity, a state ruled by a middle group of citizens between rich and poor.

Monarchy, in Aristotle's eyes, wasn't all bad. A king who governed according to reason and for the good of all people could create a good state. Yet Aristotle recognized three pitfalls of kingship. One was the hereditary nature of most monarchies. No matter how good a particular monarch might be, sooner or later a bad or incompetent ruler was bound to appear among his descendants. Another pitfall was the constant challenge of ruling unselfishly. A king should rule as a public duty, not to satisfy his own ambitions or desires, but the temptation to abuse power was great. Finally, a monarch had to rely for personal safety on armed bodyguards or even an army, and it would be all too easy for a king to turn this force into a tool of tyranny. To safeguard the public well-being, Aristotle concluded, kings should have to obey laws that would prevent them from having absolute power.

Aristotle's ideas about kingship were probably shaped by personal knowledge of kings. His life was intertwined with that of the most famous monarch of the ancient Greek world. Aristotle was a tutor and friend to Alexander, prince of Macedon, a kingdom north of Greece. Aristotle's pupil would later be known as Alexander the Great, conqueror of Greece, Turkey, Mesopotamia, Egypt, Persia, and lands beyond. Alexander became an emperor, and he also claimed divine or godlike qualities for himself. His rule was an imperial despotism that was very different from the earlier Mycenaean monarchy of warrior chieftains. Some scholars use the term Macedonian to describe Alexander's model of monarchy.

## FROM KING TO EMPEROR

Ancient Rome began as a monarchy and then became a republic. After five centuries as a republic, Rome returned to a monarchic form of government for the next five hundred years of its existence, when it was known as the Roman empire.

The early Roman monarchy had some features that were rare in the ancient world. As in many other monarchies, the king was the chief military commander and also the chief religious official. He did not, however, have absolute power. He ruled with the support and advice of a senate. This senate possessed real power, because it appointed the kings. There was no hereditary succession. When a king died, the senate chose a new king, who would rule for life. Kings, in turn, chose the senate members, all of whom came from aristocratic families. This comfortable arrangement—senators picking kings, and kings picking senators—lasted for a century or so, until the kings became power-hungry and oppressive. They began stripping power from the senate. One king, Tarquin, managed to establish a hereditary dynasty that produced the last three monarchs of the Roman kingdom. In 510 BCE the aristocrats of Rome rebelled against the king and drove him away. Having had enough of monarchy, they decided to try something else. The result was the Roman republic.

The complex government of the republic blended elements of democracy, aristocracy, and even monarchy. The aristocratic senate and various citizen assemblies passed laws and elected state officials. Instead of a monarch, the republic had two consuls, who were elected to office and ruled together for one year. As heads of state, the consuls performed some duties of the former kings, such as being commanders-in-chief of the military forces, determining how public money was spent, and representing Rome in relations with other states. The most powerful office in Rome, though, was that of dictator, a supreme military commander appointed by the senate. The post of dictator was supposed to be filled only in drastic emergencies, when Rome needed a strong central leader, and a dictator was supposed to hold office for no longer than six months. Dictatorship, however, proved to be the path by which monarchy returned to Rome.

In the first century BCE, a series of civil wars frayed the fabric of the republic. A popular and successful general named Julius Caesar took power in Rome in 48 BCE, naming himself dictator for life. He changed the structure of government in ways that took power away from the senate and assemblies and concentrated it in the central authority—himself. Caesar was assassinated in 44 BCE, but slightly more than a decade later his nephew and heir Octavian came to power. Octavian commanded Caesar's legions of soldiers, and, like Caesar, he was popular with the common people of Rome. Like Caesar, Octavian made changes in the government, but he moved more slowly, and he claimed to be preserving the traditions of the republic, not undoing them. In 27 BCE, the senate gave Octavian the title *imperator*, or emperor. Under the name Augustus Caesar, wielding more political and military power than any Roman before him, he launched Rome into its imperial era.

# The Greeks Had a Word for It

*Monarch* and *monarchy* are among the many English words that come from Greek roots—in this case, from the Greek words *monos*, or "one," and *archein*, "to rule." *Archein* became the suffix *-archy*, meaning "rule by." It appears on the ends of other political terms, such as *anarchy*, which means "rule by no one," or an absence of government.

Many words in the language of political theory owe their origin to the Greeks. *Tyranny* and *tyrant*, for example, come from the Greek word *tyrannos*, which referred to someone who ruled with absolute power and was not restrained by law. Even the word *politics* is rooted in the Greek *polis*, or organized community. One of the most useful Greek contributions to political language was *-kratia*, a suffix that, when added to another word, meant "form of government." (It's no accident that *-kratia* comes from the word *kratos*, meaning "strength" or "power." The Greeks recognized that government is defined by who holds the power.) As *-cracy*, meaning "government by," this Greek term appears in words that still shape political speech today, from the orations of world leaders to discussions at the corner coffeehouse. One such word is *democracy*, which means "government by the people"—usually understood to mean "government by the majority of the people."

From the time of the ancient Greeks to the present, political theorists have coined scores of words to describe real or imagined forms of government. Among them are:

**andrarchy, androcracy** government by men
**aristocracy** government by the aristocrats, or nobility
**autarchy** government by an autocrat, or absolute ruler
**bureaucracy** government by civil servants
**ethnocracy** government by one ethnic group
**gerontocracy** government by the old

**gynarchy, gynocracy** government by women
**kakistocracy** government by the worst
**kleptocracy** government by thieves
**matriarchy** government by women (literally, by mothers)
**meritocracy** government by the best qualified
**ochlocracy** government by mobs
**oligarchy** government by the few
**patriarchy** government by men (literally, by fathers)
**plutocracy** government by the rich
**technocracy** government by those with technical or
  scientific skills
**theocracy** government by religious law or religious leaders
**timocracy** government by landowners; also, government
  based on honor

But why let political theorists have all the fun? People have used the handy suffixes *-archy* and *-cracy* to create new words in all kinds of settings. For example, pampered domestic animals around whom whole households revolve have been called *catarchs*. People who base their voting and political actions on rainforest conservation and other ecological causes are sometimes called *envirocrats*. And a few rock musicians have referred to the early twenty-first century music industry as "the hiphopocracy."

The Roman empire covered a much wider realm than the old kingdom of Rome. Through conquest or treaty, Rome had absorbed many nations and peoples. Its emperors, like the Great Kings of the ancient Middle East, were super-monarchs who ruled over lesser kings and princes. Of course, even the most diligent, hard-working emperor could not manage such a large realm—and many of the Roman emperors were far from diligent. Over the centuries, much of the day-to-day business of running the empire was carried out by a bureaucracy, a body of civil servants, or government officials and employees.

The fortunes of the empire rose and fell with the quality of its rulers. Some were disastrously bad, such as the cruel and oppressive Nero, whose assassination in 68 CE led to another outbreak of civil war. In contrast, under a series of five good emperors between 96 and 180, Rome experienced the longest peaceful period in its history. But after the assassination in 192 of another abusive emperor, Commodus, the empire entered a long period of conflict. Rivals for the throne assassinated each other. Armies overthrew emperors they didn't like and placed their own generals on the throne, and many of these new rulers were overthrown in turn. The rate of imperial turnover was tremendous—in just a century, Rome had twenty-six emperors.

Diocletian, who became emperor in 284, restructured the imperial government. Thinking that a division of power might reduce the conflict, he designed an unusual monarchic arrangement: the empire was divided into eastern and western sections, each with a senior and a junior emperor. The senior emperors would rule for ten years, then retire. The junior emperors would become senior emperors and begin training their own junior emperors. But after Diocletian died in 305, the new order that he had designed was quickly forgotten. Strong-willed leaders once again fought for control of the entire empire. That empire would soon come to an end, although new monarchies would spring up in its place across Europe. And both before and after Rome's imperial era, kingship took a variety of forms in other parts of the world.

# Dynastic Developments Around the World **3** ■ ■ ■

GREECE ABANDONED MONARCHY and experimented with other forms of government, only to be dominated by the imperial monarchy of Alexander. Rome changed from a kingdom into a republic, only to change back into an empire. Apart from a few striking exceptions, the institution of monarchy seemed for a long time to be part of the natural order of things, and not just in the Middle East and Europe. "Of all the forms of civil organization throughout the entire sweep of human experience," writes historian W. M. Spellman in his survey of world monarchies, "the rule of a single person over a political and territorial unit has been the most widespread and the most enduring." Before the modern era, single-person rule almost always meant monarchy.

Monarchies have existed in every inhabited continent. Although all monarchies have shared some basic features, each has been shaped by its unique historical, social, and even geographic circumstances. In Europe, Asia, Africa, the Islamic world, and the Americas, monarchy took a great variety of forms.

## ASIAN MONARCHIES

"Never have so few ruled for so long over so many," wrote John King Fairbank, a leading scholar of Chinese history. He was referring to China's imperial government, one of the longest-lasting monarchies

**Chinese emperor Qin Shi Huangdi united China in an imperial state that lasted more than a thousand years.**

in world history. For more than a thousand years, this monarchy did much more than organize and run the country. It had great religious importance and, according to many scholars, it was a key symbol of Chinese identity. Spellman has claimed that "there is perhaps no more outstanding feature of Chinese culture than the longevity and stability of the imperial office."

The Chinese people traditionally pictured the roots of their civilization as entwined with the ideals of kingship. Five great rulers, according to one story about China's origins, governed the land long ago. From these mythical kings came the foundations of Chinese culture: hunting, agriculture, writing, the making of boats and silk, and the shared beliefs that underlay the social order of families, communities, and the state.

The known history of China, however, begins around 1700 BCE, with the Shang Dynasty of northern China. This royal house seems to have emerged from a background of many small states and kingdoms that were often in conflict with one another. Shang warriors conquered territory on their frontiers, enlarging the realm ruled by their monarchs. For a time the Shang kingdom was China's largest and most powerful, but around 1050 BCE, a rival kingdom called Zhou toppled the Shang and took over their territory. Although the Zhou Dynasty remained in power for centuries, the kingdom lost part of its territory to invading barbarians from the deserts on the western border. Zhou eventually fell apart into more than 170 small states and kingdoms. For several hundred years, as these warring states fought among themselves, the more powerful among them defeated and absorbed the less powerful. By about 350 BCE the state known as Qin had become the largest and strongest.

As kingdoms rose and fell throughout this period of more than a thousand years, the dynasties that rose to power—and the people they governed—held the same ideas about kingship. One of the most important concerned the relationship between the ruler and the spiritual world. As early as the Shang era, the Chinese had believed that kings had the power to communicate with such beings as gods and dead ancestors. The Shang kings practiced divination, seeking supernatural answers from the gods and ancestors to questions about the welfare of the kingdom. Rulers were also believed to be able to influence the spirits. For example, kings had to perform rituals that were supposed to ensure the good will of the gods and spirits, who in turn would favor the people with good weather, fertile soil, abundant crops, and victory over their enemies. Upon the king rested the responsibility for maintaining the proper relationship between earth and heaven.

By the time of the Zhou Dynasty, the Chinese expressed their beliefs about the connection between their earthly rulers and the divine realm with the term *tianming*, which means the mandate, or will, of heaven. Kings were said to rule by the mandate of heaven—they were appointed and supported by the gods. The king was called the *tianzi*, the Son of Heaven. If a king lost his throne, the people believed that he had lost it because the gods had withdrawn their mandate. On the other hand, if the people experienced enough disasters, such as crop failures or military defeats, they might start to think that their king was losing the mandate. And if enough people came to think that, the king could find himself suddenly out of power, with a rival ruling in his place.

Also part of Chinese culture from ancient times was the belief that the family, not the individual, is the basic unit of society. This belief had important effects on ideas about rulership. Chinese culture placed a very high value on respect for one's ancestors and for tradition. It also valued complete obedience to the head of one's family. Transferred from private to public life, these virtues set the standard for relations between the rulers and the ruled. Just as a father was to be honored and obeyed by everyone in his household, the king was to be honored and obeyed by every one of his subjects. Like the father within his household, the ruler was considered to be the source of all wisdom and authority within the country. These ideas about family and state found expression in Confucianism, a Chinese ethical system, or set of principles to guide behavior.

A turning point for the Chinese monarchy came in 221 BCE, when a Qin ruler replaced the title *wang* (king) with *huangdi* (emperor). Qin Shi Huangdi, as he was known, was the first to unite much of modern China under a single rule. The imperial state he established endured for more than a thousand years, surviving civil wars, rebellions, attacks from barbarian enemies, and long periods of unrest. On a few occasions women held the throne, but their times in power were viewed as exceptional cases. Perhaps because of the influence of Confucianism, the proper monarch in Chinese culture and tradition was an emperor, not an empress.

The Chinese empire remained, but dynasties came and went. Historian Spellman points to "a pattern of dynastic change always present in the history of the Chinese monarchy." Dynasties were founded by aggressive, successful generals or warlords. These rulers and their early successors were usually both active and capable. Many were good administrators as well as good generals. As each dynasty experienced generations of peace and prosperity, however, the later rulers grew detached from the problems and challenges of managing their large empire. Pampered and isolated, they turned responsibility over to their advisers and the palace staff. In time, the empire fell prey to rebellion or attack. Eventually a new aggressor seized the throne and founded a new dynasty. Yet each time a dynasty fell or was overthrown, the new one that rose up had much the same form, continuing the imperial state under a new family and a new name. Even foreign conquerors who invaded China and established their own dynasties there—Mongols from the northwest in the thirteenth century and Manchus from the northeast in the seventeenth century—kept the imperial administration and rituals largely intact.

What made the Chinese monarchy so long-lasting and stable? Some of the continuity of the imperial state can be traced to its founder, Qin Shi Huangdi, who was determined to unify the vast and varied empire. He strengthened imperial authority by enlarging the army, he built roads and canals to link far-flung parts of the empire, and he revised legal codes so that all parts of the empire had the same laws. He caused weights, measures, and coinage to be standardized throughout the empire, replacing the many different systems of measurements and monetary units that people had used in various states. All of these measures served to weld China together, making it easier to rule.

One of Qin Shi Huangdi's most significant steps was to create an administrative organization to run the empire under his command. He divided China into forty-eight districts. For each he appointed a military commander and a civilian minister, and each of these had many other levels beneath him. Over the centuries, this civilian administrative system would become a highly organized civil-service bureaucracy. Unlike aristocracies based on noble birth, the Chinese civil service was a meritocracy, based on performance. Anyone who hoped to enter the civil service had to receive a good education and pass many tests. Even commoners, however, could advance in the system, if they distinguished themselves in their studies. The course of study that prepared students for civil-service exams was based on Confucian writings, which emphasized order, obedience to authority, and the need to act always in the best interests of the state.

Civil-service officials were responsible for every aspect of life in imperial China, from law and education to mining and tax collection. The emperor depended on the bureaucrats to get things done—but the bureaucracy depended on the imperial state for its very existence. With few exceptions, the scholar-officials of the bureaucracy were noted for their loyalty to the emperor. And even when they supported a change of dynasties, they resisted any attempt to alter the form or structure of government. "Confucian officials took their duties seriously," historian W. J. F. Jenner has written, "including their loyalty both to the throne and to the whole system of values in which they had been educated and that gave their careers meaning."

Outside China, monarchies rose and fell in many parts of Asia, including India, Southeast Asia, and the steppes of Central Asia. But the empire that emerged in the islands of Japan proved to be unusually long-lasting. Although the Japanese monarchy shared some features with China's imperial state, in other ways it reflected Japan's distinctive culture. The ups and downs of the Japanese empire show that rulership and power can go separate ways.

Japanese tradition says that the empire was founded around 660 BCE by Jinmu, the first emperor, who was a descendant of the sun goddess, Amaterasu. History, however, dates the beginning of the Japanese monarchy to about the sixth century CE.

For centuries before that time, Japan was divided among hundreds of *uji*, or clans. Everyone in a clan was related by blood and worshipped the same deity, who was associated with an ancestor. Each clan was headed by its warrior aristocrats. Leadership of a clan stayed within a single family and was handed down from father to son. As in many other cultures, a clan leader had responsibilities in both the political and spiritual realms. He was the clan's military commander and its chief priest. Over time, one clan in Yamato, a region in the southeastern part of Honshu island, absorbed or conquered other clans around it. By the sixth century, the Yamato clan was powerful enough, and its territory large enough, to be called a kingdom.

In 645 CE the Yamato king issued a statement called the Taika Reform Edict. This royal order reorganized the monarchy along lines borrowed from the Chinese imperial system. Japan's monarchy was now an empire headed by an autocrat who claimed absolute power as well as ownership of all of the land in the realm. The emperor was also the high priest, said to have been appointed by the gods to rule.

Japan's imperial dynasty now traced its ancestry to Jinmu and the sun goddess Amaterasu. When rulers of Japan wrote to rulers of China, they mentioned their connection with the goddess, calling themselves "emperors of the rising sun." The rising sun is still a Japanese national symbol.

Adopting the Confucian image of the state as a large family, the Yamato emperors presented themselves as the fathers of their people. They wanted to create a Chinese-style bureaucracy based on Confucian ideals of service. That plan, however, did not sit well with Japan's powerful clan leaders and aristocrats, many of whom were scattered through remote parts of the countryside. They were used to a high degree of independence in regional affairs, and they did not cooperate with efforts to impose a strong, centralized, Chinese-style government. Instead, Japan became something of a two-part empire—one part theory, and one part reality. In theory, the emperor was the supreme authority, and everyone acknowledged that authority. But in reality, local and regional overlords strengthened their own power. They did not always send the taxes they collected on to the imperial treasury, and they doled out land within their regions—land that supposedly belonged to the emperor—to their own followers, in order to build up bands of loyal supporters.

Over time, one powerful clan after another rose to power by marrying into the imperial family, taking over key administrative positions in the empire, and creating a private army. By the twelfth century, the emperor had been reduced to little more than a symbol. He performed ceremonies but had no real power. That state of affairs continued for centuries. The emperor remained the official but powerless ruler of the land even after a branch of the royal family set up a separate government called the Ashikaga Shogunate in the fourteenth century. War broke out among rivals within the Ashikaga Shogunate, and by the sixteenth century the empire had fragmented into several hundred small states ruled by *daimyos*, or regional warlords.

Remarkably, Japan's monarchy did not disappear during these centuries of strife and power-grabbing. Not only did the monarchy survive, but the original dynasty remained on the imperial throne. In China, if a general or warlord managed to usurp the throne and start a new dynasty, the takeover was interpreted as a sign that the mandate of heaven had moved. But in Japan, the emperor was believed to be descended from the gods, not just appointed by them. Even in times of civil war, the Japanese placed a high value on keeping the royal line of descent unbroken. It was their connection to the divine.

Japan's first contact with Europeans came in 1543, when Portuguese explorer-traders arrived in the islands. Soon afterward, a capable general named Toyotomi Hideyoshi, who saw a need for Japan to protect itself against the outside world, launched the fractured empire into a new era of strong, centralized government. Through conquest and alliance he brought more and more of the small states under his control, although he made a great point of claiming to rule in the emperor's name. This practice continued under the Tokugawa Shogunate, which held most of the power in Japan from 1603 to 1867.

The Tokugawa shoguns, or rulers, always acknowledged the political and spiritual authority of the emperors. The shoguns claimed to be merely the emperors' regents or servants. They restored imperial glory by filling the royal treasury and rebuilding the palaces. At the same time, though, they kept the emperors isolated from the public and from most members of the court. No one could approach the god-emperor without the shogun's permission. In this way the shoguns strengthened the institution of monarchy while keeping real power out of the hands of the monarch.

## MUSLIM MONARCHIES

The religion known as Islam was founded in Arabia in the seventh century by a merchant-turned-prophet named Muhammad. Within a few centuries the Muslims, or followers of the new faith, had spread Islam across a broad swath of the known world, from Africa and Spain to India and central Asia. Bringing scores of peoples into a single form of worship, they created a civilization that was the most ethnically and culturally diverse of its time but was unified by a shared religion. Out of this "powerful and dynamic form of political and religious authority," as historian W. M. Spellman has called it, new forms of monarchy would arise.

Before Islam, political organization in Arabia revolved around the *umma*, usually translated as "tribe." The *umma* was a group of clans held together by ties of kinship and loyalty. Occasionally some tribes joined together in alliances or loose federations, but there was no central authority. The birth of Islam, however, created a central authority in the figure of Muhammad. After he managed to bring an

**Tokogawa Yoshinobu, Japan's last shogun, holds a fan as he sits on the humble perch that belies his vast influence.**

end to fighting between clans in the city of Medina, he became the city's political leader. This took place in 622 CE, which is the year 1 in the calendar used today by millions of Muslims worldwide.

As Islam grew, Muhammad's political authority expanded along with it. Although clan and kin remained important, the primary allegiance of Muslims was to their faith. The old *umma* remained the model of political organization, but now all Muslims belonged to a single, large, ever-growing *umma* of fellow believers. Their sovereign and prophet were one and the same. This Muslim community was a theocratic monarchy, a type of kingdom in which the political and religious leaders and organizations are identical, and which is governed according to religious laws. When other peoples and states came under the sway of Islam and its Arab rulers, the monarchy grew into an empire.

Muhammad died in 632. After his death, the political and spiritual leader of the Muslims was called the caliph. The caliphate—the position of the caliph—endured into the modern era, but it did not survive unchanged. Over the span of centuries, two opposing forces shaped the history of the Muslim empire. One force was the belief that all Muslims of the world should be united in a single political organization, as they were already united in religion. The opposing force was disunity, caused by ethnic and cultural differences, by the difficulty of managing an empire across vast distances, and by internal conflict.

The first crisis arose within a few years of the prophet's death, when disagreement over the succession to the caliphate led to war. Muhammad had left no instructions about who should lead the Muslims after him, or how Muslims should choose their leader. At first, the elite warriors who had been Muhammad's companions chose the caliphs by acclamation, a show of personal approval and support. Soon, though, those who favored acclamation as the means of succession came into violent conflict with those who felt that the caliph had to be descended from Muhammad's clan. A schism occurred, splitting the Muslim faith into separate, rival groups, the Sunni and Shi'ite Muslims—a division that persists today. The Sunni, who originally favored acclamation, have always been in the majority.

By 661, the governor of Syria had been recognized as caliph. Although he was a Sunni, he adopted the principle of hereditary succession, to the benefit of his descendants. He founded the Umayyad

Dynasty, which produced fourteen caliphs. The Umayyads borrowed some administrative methods, such as tax systems, from empires that had flourished in Persia (now Iran) and elsewhere. The next dynasty, the Abbasids, held the caliphate from 750 to 1258. Baghdad, in what is now Iraq, was their capital. Spiritual leadership and sovereignty, once united in the person of Muhammad, drifted apart under the Abbasids. The Muslim theocratic monarchy began to become fragmented.

As early as the first century of Islam, scholar-judges who specialized in interpreting religious laws had insisted that their authority in spiritual and religious matters was equal to that of the caliphs. During the Abbasid era, scholarship flourished in the Islamic empire, but the religious schools claimed increasing independence. Spiritual authority was no longer one with secular, or worldly, authority, as represented by the caliph. And that secular authority itself was crumbling. The caliphs claimed absolute power, but numerous quarrels over succession disrupted the caliphate. So did regional rebellions against central rule. By 945, when Shi'ites from Persia invaded Baghdad, the caliph was more figurehead than ruler. Real power lay with the regents, warlords, and chieftains who ruled various parts of the Islamic world, claiming to do so in the emperor's name. One Muslim general even conquered northern India and, declaring himself independent of the caliphate, made himself sultan, or king, of a new monarchy there.

The caliphate survived, but in weakened form. The vision of a single, united state for all Muslims was a dream of the past. Instead, after about 1400, three new Muslim empires emerged: the Ottoman Turks in Turkey and North Africa, the Safavid dynasty in Persia, and the Mughals in India. Each of these empires was ruled by an absolute monarch, although only one of those monarchs—the Ottoman sultan— also claimed to be the caliph, or leader of the faith for all Muslims. Each of the three empires experienced conflicts over succession to the throne, as well as war with other Islamic states.

The Ottomans were Turkic peoples who originated on the plains of central Asia. According to Turkic custom, legitimacy—or the right to the throne—passed from generation to generation within a single ruling family. Yet the Turks did not adopt primogeniture, which is the practice of making the oldest son the heir. As a result, any one of a king's sons could become the next king. Rival claims were common. Brothers frequently came into conflict over who would inherit their

**This Safavid painting depicts an elephant made of men. The armies commanded by the Safavid shahs used elephants in warfare.**

father's kingship. In a way, Islam made matters worse, at least as far as royal succession was concerned. When the Ottomans adopted Islam, they also adopted the Islamic practice of marrying more than one wife. This meant that a king would have even more male offspring to compete with each other for his throne. The death of a ruler could bring on a mass of claims, counterclaims, plots, and palace coups.

Sultan Mehmed II, who ruled the empire from 1451 to 1481, took a harsh approach to ending the confusion. He introduced the "law of fratricide," or brother killing. Under this law, each new sultan picked the one male relative he thought best suited to succeed him—then killed the rest. The sultan called Selim the Grim, for example, killed all of his brothers and nephews and all but one of his sons. That son, Suleiman, became sultan in turn, and in turn he killed two of his three sons. Sultans followed this practice until 1595, when Mehmed III had nineteen brothers executed. He also had a number of pregnant women killed to prevent their unborn children from becoming claimants to the throne.

The Safavids were a dynasty of Persian Shi'ites who extended their rule beyond Persia. In 1508 the Safavid monarch—called the shah—conquered Baghdad, which had been the capital of Sunni caliphs in earlier times. A few years later the Safavids encouraged a rebellion of Shi'ite subjects in the eastern part of the Ottoman empire, and a Persian army invaded Ottoman territory. The Ottoman sultan turned back the shah's army and ended the invasion, but hostility remained between Persian Shi'ites and Ottoman Sunnis.

On the opposite side of Persia from the Ottoman empire, in the east, another Sunni power rose in India. As early as the eleventh century, Muslim invaders from the north and west had conquered parts of northern India and set themselves up as rulers. By the early thirteenth century these Muslim states had merged into a sultanate, with its capital at Delhi. From there, Muslim monarchs ruled over a large population that continued to follow the Hindu religion. Muslims remained a very tiny minority. The Delhi sultanate never became a theocratic monarchy like the Ottoman and Safavid states, where the ruler embodied the faith of most of his subjects. Instead, the sultan ruled through a large number of Hindu kings and princes. They kept their thrones and titles in exchange for promising allegiance to the sultan.

The Delhi sultanate lasted for several centuries and five dynasties. It eventually crumbled, but it had created a model for the rule of India by foreign Muslims. In the fifteenth century, a new wave of raiders entered India from Afghanistan. They were Sunni Muslims who overthrew the last of the Delhi sultans and founded a new state called the Mughal empire. The empire reached its largest extent under the third emperor, Akbar, who ruled from 1556 to 1605. He created a large, efficient monarchy with a high degree of ethnic and religious diversity.

Like the Delhi sultans, Akbar allowed native Indian kings to keep their territories and titles, as long as they turned the real power of government over to him and his officials. He filled the imperial administration and the army with people from many ethnic backgrounds and religious faiths: Persian Shi'ites, Sunni Afghans and Uzbeks from central Asia, and native Indians who followed the Muslim, Hindu, Buddhist, Jain, Parsee, and Sikh faiths. In order to keep any one group from gaining enough power to threaten his rule, he brought members of all groups into the aristocracy. Akbar married a Hindu princess and encouraged his high-ranking nobles to do the same. Through law and example, he promoted religious tolerance, donating money to Hindu temples and celebrating Hindu holidays. He even tried to establish a new belief system called Din-i-Illah, which added elements from other religions to a Muslim core. These acts brought scorn from the Muslim scholar-judges, who considered themselves to be the true interpreters of Islam. Their anger increased in 1579, when Akbar issued an imperial edict saying that the ruler's decision in matters of religious law carried greater weight than that of the scholar-judges. In effect, Akbar had declared that the king was the ultimate religious authority.

Akbar was an autocrat, a monarch who kept the reins of power firmly in his own hands. Because he was also capable, charismatic, and energetic, he ruled successfully. His successors, unfortunately, shared neither his vision for the empire nor his ability to run it. And as in the Ottoman empire, succession itself was a problem. The Mughals, like the Ottomans, often tried to solve the succession problem with bloodshed.

In 1602 Akbar's oldest son, Selim, led a revolt against his father, hoping to seize the throne. Three years later, Selim got the throne after his father died—possibly poisoned by Selim. Ruling under the name Jahangir, Akbar's heir endured not one but many revolts by his own son. Finally, Jahangir blinded and imprisoned the young man. Another emperor, Shah Jahan, celebrated his rise to power in 1627 by slaughtering nearly all of his male relatives. His son, Aurangzeb, did the same when he took the throne by force thirty years later. Aurangzeb threw Shah Jahan into prison and killed his own brothers.

None of Akbar's heirs had shared his commitment to religious tolerance, but Aurangzeb was determined to restore Islam to what he believed was its rightful place as the primary religion of the empire. He passed laws that persecuted Hindus, he executed a Sikh leader for refusing to become a Muslim, and he tried to enforce Islamic religious law on the entire population. In response, Hindus and Sikhs launched revolts against Mughal rule. When Aurangzeb died in 1707, his sons fought over the throne. The winner, following family tradition, killed the losers. By this time, the British were in India, forming alliances with various Hindu states. These alliances threatened the already weakened Mughal empire. Then, in 1739, a Shi'ite Persian force swept down on the Mughal capital. "Ignoring all notions of Muslim brotherhood," as historian W. M. Spellman writes, "the invaders looted Delhi, massacred 30,000 inhabitants, and removed the imperial Peacock throne, commissioned by Shah Jahan, to Persia." Invaders from Afghanistan followed a few years later.

The Mughal empire never recovered from these blows. It fragmented into many small states, some Hindu, some Muslim. By the end of the eighteenth century, the former Mughal territory was being taken over, bit by bit, by the British.

## AFRICAN MONARCHIES

Monarchies in Africa took many forms, from loose associations like clusters of chieftainships to large states ruled by autocrats with massive armies. The basis for all of these monarchies, however, was a pattern of village life that was widespread across the continent south of the Sahara Desert. Key elements of village life were custom or tradition, kinship or blood relationships, and communal decision making and ownership of property. Authority at the village level rested with the elders of each lineage (an extended family that shared a common ancestor). Larger villages were headed by chieftains. A chieftain might be the oldest member of the community, the most successful hunter or warrior, or possibly the recognized religious leader.

In time, kinship relations at the village level started broadening into larger associations of people. This happened around 900 CE in many parts of the continent, although in some places it happened

**Mughal emperor Akbar I ran the Ottoman empire through a combination of energy and fierce control. Akbar II, along with his other sons, did not have the same power.**

earlier and in others it did not happen until much later. Groups of lineages that were linked by intermarriage joined together into clans or tribes, perhaps for protection against other groups that were getting larger, or simply so that people could hunt and farm on a larger scale. The clans in turn combined to form new, larger unions, some of which became monarchies. Heads of the lineages and chieftains of the clans were then subject to an overall leader, a king.

In most African monarchies, kings did not inherit their thrones. Instead, the monarchs were selected by the most powerful and respected chieftains. The choice of a new king and the transfer of power did not always go smoothly—armed conflicts over succession were common. Victory was seen as a sign that the triumphant warrior would make a good king.

Kings were almost always notable military leaders, but military command was only one of a king's responsibilities. Monarchs were also expected to carry out rituals and ceremonies to protect the spiritual health of the people. Most of these rituals involved making offerings to the spirits of ancestors, or communicating with them. These ancestral spirits were thought to link the human world with the divine. African kings, while not usually thought of as gods themselves, were supposed to exist in a state of being higher than that of ordinary men and women because of their constant connection with the ancestors and the spirit world. In some African kingdoms, monarchs were killed or committed suicide when they became old and sick; their weaknesses made them unsuitable to serve as links to the spirits.

Because African monarchies began as enlargements of kinship groups, and because a ruler's most trusted and loyal followers were his kin, family relationships could make or break a king. No factor was more important in building those relationships than marriage— specifically, polygyny, the practice of marrying multiple wives. In most African cultures, any man could marry more than one wife, but few men had more than two or three. Chieftains had more wives, perhaps dozens. Kings had even more. For monarchs, marriage was a way to form and cement new kinship bonds. They liked to marry into each of the lineages in their kingdoms, so the larger the kingdom, the greater the number of wives. In addition, when kings conquered other peoples and absorbed their territories, they generally married into the royal or chieftain families of their new subjects. A monarch could end up married to hundreds or, in rare cases, thousands of women.

These multiple marriages produced a great many offspring. Royal sons were often destined to become warriors, soldiers, and chieftains. Royal daughters could be married to men in other important families as another way of reinforcing kinship connections.

The largest kingdoms developed where trade flourished, bringing wealth that monarchs were eager to control. Ghana, located in western Africa at a crossroads of trade routes for gold, salt, pepper, and ivory, was one of the first of these powerful monarchies. It appears in Islamic writings as early as the ninth century. At its height, Ghana was the largest known African empire, covering 193,050 square miles (500,000 square kilometers). Its king, an autocrat viewed by his people as almost godlike, was the chief judge, priest, and military commander of the realm.

Near the end of the eleventh century, Muslim conquerors made Islam a driving force in Ghana. Other kingdoms that later appeared in Africa just south of the Sahara, such as Mali and Songhai, were also Muslim states. Islam introduced a new element to African monarchy: the idea that it was a ruler's duty to see that the state promoted God's will, which was that all people should be Muslims. At first, only the kings, councilors, aristocrats, and other elite members of society adopted Islam. The large mass of peasants and villagers continued to practice their traditional religions. Over time, however, Islam became more deeply rooted in the general population.

Unlike large, highly organized empires such as the Chinese and Ottoman states, the kingdoms of Ghana, Mali, and Songhai—called the Sudanic kingdoms—did not have elaborate bureaucracies, firm borders, or even uniform codes of law. Within each region of one of these empires, chieftains and village leaders maintained order and law according to local tradition. The people's main responsibility to their sovereign was to pay tribute in the form of food, ivory, gold, or other valuable goods. The monarch used the tribute to pay for his army and court. An army was necessary, for rulers frequently had to rely on force to keep rebellious chieftains and their subjects in line. Succession, too, was a perpetual problem—one that was often solved violently. Rival warriors, ambitious chieftains, and the many sons of kings fought for the thrones.

The last of the Sudanic kingdoms, Songhai, had fallen apart by the seventeenth century. Meanwhile, other kingdoms had risen and fallen. In the east, along the coast of the Indian Ocean, a string of small monarchies formed. Deeply influenced by Islam, economically dependent on trade across the Indian Ocean, states such as Zanzibar were ruled by sultans but were often little larger than cities or small islands. A much larger state developed inland, in what is now Zimbabwe. It left impressive stone ruins and the remains of extensive gold mines, but no written records. Almost nothing is known of the political organization of Great Zimbabwe, as the largest group of ruins is called, although the writings of a few Portuguese explorers and traders say that it was ruled by a powerful king who controlled the gold trade.

The kingdoms of western Africa, in present-day Angola, Congo, and Nigeria, are slightly better known. Some of the most detailed European accounts concern the kingdom of Kongo, in Angola. Established through conquest, Kongo had an army and a system of tribute like those of the Sudanic kingdoms. The king's power was limited, however; he made decisions jointly with a set of advisors and lineage heads. These same councilors chose the kings, although monarchs always came from the ruling family. Like most African kingdoms, Kongo had no formal system of succession to indicate which family member should be chosen as the next monarch. When a king died, fighting usually broke out among his potential heirs and their supporters.

After 1500 or so, the European presence increased in Africa south of the Sahara. Before long, Europeans were principally concerned with developing the trade in slaves. Old monarchies based on the control of trade routes and natural resources collapsed or withered away. New states arose to exploit the new market in slaves for sale to the Europeans. The Asante kingdom in western Africa is one example. It was closely tied to European slave-trading interests, and much of the king's income came from selling slaves. The Asante monarch had no autocratic power. Instead, he ruled at the will of the clan chieftains who selected him and kept him in power. He was more symbol than ruler. As in other African monarchies, the basis of the Asante kingdom was not the abstract idea of kingship itself but the power of the clan.

## AMERICAN MONARCHIES

Europeans arrived in the Americas in the late fifteenth century. Soon they were colonizing the newly located continents, imposing their

# The Warrior
# Queen of Angola

Women have occupied the thrones of monarchs. They have ruled their people in times of war, and sometimes they have even led their armies into battle. In *The Warrior Queens* (1988), British historian and biographer Antonia Fraser described the deeds and historical significance of a dozen of these military female monarchs. One was Boudicca or Boadicea, who led her native Britons in a rebellion against Roman rule in the first century CE. Tamara, who was queen of Georgia from 1184 to 1212, conducted military campaigns that turned her kingdom east of the Black Sea into a small empire.

A remarkable African queen named Jinga (or Zhinga) Mbandi became a legend for refusing to be dominated by the Europeans who were exploiting her land during the rise of the slave trade. Jinga's life and actions are known mostly through accounts written by the Europeans with whom she had dealings. As a result, the details are sketchy and sometimes conflicting, but the basic outlines of her life and achievements are clear. Jinga Mbandi was born sometime in the 1580s in western central Africa. Her father was the king of Ndongo, one of the two main kingdoms in what is now Angola (the other was Kongo). Jinga's first appearance in history came in the early 1600s, when she became Ndongo's representative in negotiations with the Portuguese. These Europeans had arrived on the western coast of Africa more than a century earlier as explorers and missionaries. Very quickly, though, their focus had shifted to the trade in African slaves, which they needed for their fast-growing plantation colony in Brazil. By Jinga's time, Angola was a Portuguese colony. The settlement of Luanda was its capital and chief port for the shipment of slaves. The Portuguese considered Angola an ideal source of this human commodity—one official wrote, in fact, that the region would supply slaves "until the end of the world."

After Jinga's brother became king of Ndongo, the Portuguese governor of the colony exiled him. That left the job of negotiating Ndongo's independence up to Jinga. To win the favor of the Portuguese, she allowed herself to be baptized a Christian and adopted the European name Anna. Her sisters Mukumbu and Kifunji did the same, becoming Barbara and Grace. It's likely that Jinga also promised that Ndongo would not interfere with the slave trade, and she may have agreed to sell non-Ndongo captives to the Europeans—many African leaders did this to preserve their own people's freedom. At any rate, Jinga persuaded the Portuguese not just to leave Ndongo alone but even to help defend it against invaders.

In 1624 the king of Ndongo died. Rumors said that Jinga had had him killed, along with her nephew, so that she could take the throne. Whatever the truth of that suggestion, she did become queen. The Portuguese disapproved and set up a puppet king of their own choosing, someone whom they could easily control. Jinga refused to give up power, however, and many people in Ndongo remained loyal. A few years later Jinga responded to the Portuguese insult by blocking a key Portuguese trade route. Her next step was to lead her followers east, where they conquered a group called the Jagas. This victory gave Jinga more subjects and a power base farther from the Portuguese settlements. In the 1640s she attacked the Portuguese in two ways. First, she made an alliance with their rivals, the Dutch, selling them her prisoners of war. Second, she fought Portuguese forces, leading her soldiers to several victories. In battle she carried an axe and a sword and was clad as a warrior chieftain in animal skins. In 1648, however, Jinga's Dutch allies were defeated by the Portuguese, so she prudently withdrew into her eastern territory. In 1656 the elderly queen negotiated peace with the Portuguese, allowing them to carry on certain trading and missionary activities in exchange for the release of one of her sisters who had long been a Portuguese captive.

When Jinga died in 1663, her body was displayed to her subjects wrapped in royal robes—and holding weapons. Through a combination of skillful diplomacy, shrewd bargaining, and ruthless military command, Queen Jinga had held onto her people's independence and her own throne for nearly forty years.

own political structures on them. Before that time, many forms of political organization had emerged among the native peoples of the Americas. The largest and most highly organized states were a handful of monarchies in Mexico and Central and South America. North America undoubtedly had monarchies, although they would not have been large, highly structured, or bureaucratic.

In the accounts that Europeans wrote during the early centuries of contact with the native peoples of North America, certain leaders are called "kings." Yet the descriptions of these rulers and their states suggest that these kings were more like the head chieftains of tribes or groups of tribes. They did not necessarily have the power, status, or responsibility of monarchs. In most cases they do not seem to have been lawmakers or spiritual leaders, and they governed not by royal will but by the consent and agreement of the community.

To the south, however, more formally monarchic states developed between 800 BCE and 1350 CE. The Olmec, Maya, and Aztec kingdoms of Mexico and Central America and the Inca empire of Peru were theocratic monarchies. Their political structures were closely linked to religious beliefs and practices. All of these peoples built significant urban centers, clusters of large buildings, plazas, and monuments. Most of these sprawling stone ruins, from Tenochtitlàn and Chichen Itza in Mexico to Machu Picchu in Peru, are the remains of religious centers. Modern scholars think that these urban centers were inhabited by priests, royalty, nobles, soldiers, and servants. The mass of people lived outside the urban complexes in small villages, tending their farms and herds. People crowded into the centers in great numbers, however, for religious ceremonies.

The Aztec empire is a good example of how rulership can be supported by religion and myth. At the beginning of the twelfth century, a people called the Toltecs rose to power in central Mexico. The Toltecs overcame many other groups in the region and harnessed slave labor for their large-scale construction ventures. Then, around the middle of the fourteenth century, the Aztecs moved into Toltec territory from the north. The Aztecs conquered the Toltecs, taking over not just their territory and their subject peoples but elements of Toltec culture and customs as well.

Less than a century later, an Aztec ruler named Itzcóatl put forth a new version of the Aztec past. According to this new view of history, the Aztec aristocrats were descended from the Toltec royalty and the sun god Huitzilopochtli. This myth accomplished two things. First, it presented the Aztecs not as invaders but as heirs to the Toltec civilization, with a rightful claim to their lands. Second, it established a kinship between the Aztec nobility and a major deity. This was important because the king always came from the noble class, and the Aztecs wanted their ruler to embody a link between the divine and human worlds.

The Aztec monarchy passed from generation to generation within a dynasty, but there was no clear rule of succession. When a king died, the most important and powerful members of the nobility chose his successor from among his male relatives. Often they chose his oldest son, but they could choose a brother or a nephew, if no sons were suitable. The Aztec monarchs were high priests as well as rulers. They controlled an empire that at its largest contained about twenty million people, and they ruled these subjects by force. Every man had to serve in the army, and war was a way of life, because the Aztecs required a steady stream of prisoners for religious ceremonies that involved the sacrifice of hundreds, sometimes thousands, of victims at a time.

To the south, in present-day Peru and Bolivia, the Inca state took shape in the twelfth century. Within a few hundred years it had conquered peoples along the entire length of the Andes Mountains. Government in the Inca empire was more highly organized and centralized than in the Aztec state, and human sacrifice was less common. The Inca ruler's connection to the divine was even deeper than that of the Aztec monarch—the emperor was believed to be descended directly from Inti, the sun god, and was at times worshipped as a god himself.

Like the pharaohs of ancient Egypt, the Inca rulers married their sisters, in order to keep the bloodline of the god concentrated within their family. They took other wives as well. Sons born to these wives were considered royal, but not fully divine unless their mothers were royal cousins. As in monarchic courts in other parts of the world, the custom of marrying multiple wives sometimes caused trouble for the Incas. Wars could break out when rival sons claimed the throne. When the Spanish arrived in Peru in 1521, they took advantage of just such a conflict between royal claimants to seize power, bringing down the far-flung Inca empire with only one hundred and eighty men.

# 4

## The Changing Roles of European Rulers

FOR HUNDREDS OF YEARS, the Roman empire covered most of Europe, along with parts of North Africa and the Middle East. But the empire could not last forever. When it fell, its eastern portion became a highly organized, centralized, theocratic state in which the monarch had absolute power. That state endured for the next millennium. Western Europe, fractured into many competing states, followed a very different path. There, the meaning of monarchy and the rights of rulers kept changing, defined by a thousand-year tug-of-war between kings and the church, as well as by power struggles among kings, their nobles, and the people.

### ROME'S TWO HEIRS

The Roman emperor Diocletian, who reigned from 284 to 305 CE, thought that a divided empire would be easier to govern. In 293 CE he created a tetrarchy, or system of four rulers. The empire was divided into eastern and western sections, each under the rule of a senior emperor. Each section in turn was split into two regions, one administered by the senior emperor and one by his junior emperor. All Roman-controlled territory, however, was still considered a single empire.

Perhaps the tetrarchy was too unstable for Rome, given its generals' long history of competing for power. At any rate, it did not last long after Diocletian's death. His successor, Constantine, who ruled from 306

The Roman emperor Diocletian divided his empire into four parts so it would be easier to govern, but that plan didn't work out well.

to 337, brought the entire empire under his rule. Constantine did two things that profoundly changed the empire. First, he converted to the Christian religion, made Christianity lawful throughout the empire, and encouraged other Romans to adopt it. Second, he moved the imperial capital from Rome east to the ancient Greek city of Byzantium, which was renamed Constantinople and is now Istanbul.

In the years that followed, while Constantinople became the center of the empire's political life, imperial control weakened in western Europe. Barbarian invasions and general lawlessness increased. The population declined in some areas, cities shrank or were abandoned, and agriculture and trade lessened. Meanwhile, the eastern part of the empire grew populous and prosperous. Finally, in 395, Roman territory was formally divided into two separate empires. The western one was centered in Rome. The eastern one, called the Eastern Roman empire or the Byzantine empire, was centered in Constantinople.

The splitting of the old Roman empire was mirrored by a split in religion, as the Christian faith evolved into two forms. The west followed the Latin church, later called Roman Catholic. The Byzantine form came to be known as the Orthodox church. Both churches descended from early Christianity. Although they were similar in many ways, the differences between them were enough to ignite religious conflicts over the centuries.

The Byzantine empire was a theocracy. The church defined the state, and the emperor—called the basileus—was the supreme authority in both. The vision of a Christian empire gave legitimacy to the Byzantine monarchy, as explained in the writings of a bishop named Eusebius of Caesarea, who was active in the early fourth century CE. The state was supposed to be an earthly counterpart to the kingdom of heaven. One deity ruled in heaven, and therefore one monarch must rule on earth. Monarchy was the only acceptable form of government, because no other form mirrored the divine order. Over the centuries, a handful of women ruled the Byzantine empire, usually as regents for their young sons, but a male monarch—the earthly counterpart of God the Father—was standard.

As God's representative and servant on earth, the basileus was responsible for the management of the faith. The Byzantine emperors appointed the official spiritual heads of the Orthodox church, called patriarchs, and could force them to resign. Emperors also named or

## CONSTANTIN
## LE GRAND

By making Christianity lawful throughout his empire, Constantine made a change that reverberated for centuries.

approved bishops and other high church officials, ran church councils, and had the power to make or alter both church and state law.

On the secular or civilian side of his monarchy, the basileus was the head of a vast and highly structured government bureaucracy that administered law, collected taxes, and supervised the economy throughout the provinces. The Byzantine empire was the most organized and effective large government of its time, apart from China's. The basileus himself, however, had little contact with the people he ruled. Byzantine emperors lived in secluded, guarded palaces and kept out of the public eye, except at certain religious ceremonies. Loyalty and service to the basileus were expected of everyone in the empire, but for nearly all of them the emperor would remain a remote, almost mythical figure, more symbol than man.

Over its long history, the eastern Roman empire survived many attacks by the western Europeans and by other powers, including Huns, Arabs, Persians, Vikings, and Turks. The end came in 1453, when Constantinople fell to a besieging army of Muslim Turks who overthrew the Byzantine empire and established in its place a new monarchic state, the Ottoman empire.

For a thousand years before the fall of the eastern Roman empire, the Byzantines considered themselves to be the true heirs of Rome. The glory of the old empire lived on in their state. Their emperors were *augusti* (majesties), in the tradition of Octavian-turned-Augustus, the first Roman emperor, and his successors. But six and a half centuries before the fall of Constantinople, another king had claimed the title of Roman emperor. His name was Charles the Great, or Charlemagne, and he rose to power out of the chaos of western Europe.

The western Roman empire had fallen into confusion in the fifth century. A string of rulers held the throne, but their power was feeble compared to that of the old Roman emperors or the Byzantine monarchs. Under almost constant attack by barbarian kings, chieftains, and warlords, the Western empire finally collapsed in 476 when a Germanic king named Odoacer seized the throne from Romulus Augustus, the last Roman ruler.

By that time, much of Rome's former territory in western Europe was occupied by Germanic tribes—the Vandals, Angles, Goths, Visigoths, Ostrogoths, and others—who had migrated through the region over several centuries. They formed dozens of small kingdoms.

Several key features of these Germanic kingdoms would shape the development of monarchy in Europe.

Germanic kingship was tribal, not territorial. The Germanic peoples were frequently in movement, migrating from place to place in search of new conquests or to escape conflict. This way of life meant that a king ruled over his followers, not over a territory with fixed borders. Eventually, the Germanic peoples became more or less settled. For some time, however, they continued to define kingship as having command over a population rather than as controlling a tract of land. The territorial concept of monarchy did eventually take hold, but slowly, over hundreds of years, as borders within Europe started to become fixed instead of fluid.

Kingship and kinship were inseparable for the Germanic peoples. Each of the main tribes was made up of many clans, or sets of closely related families. The leaders of each clan were its senior and most successful warriors. The king generally came from the most powerful clan—not necessarily the largest, but the one that commanded the most respect from the tribe as a whole.

The Germans elected their kings, choosing them by acclamation. But rulers who came to power through personal approval and support could lose power if that support disappeared. Military defeats, famines, or other misfortunes for the tribe could result in a king being overthrown, and possibly killed. Kingship then passed to a different clan. On the other hand, as long as the fortunes of the tribe remained reasonably good, kingship would likely remain within one clan. The king would choose his successor from among his descendants, but the tribe's acclamation was needed to seal the succession.

Just as European concepts of monarchy slowly changed from tribal to territorial, the means of succession changed, too. Many monarchies that originally elected their kings—even if the chosen kings tended to come from the ruling family more often than not—gradually became hereditary monarchies. In these states, it was taken for granted that the heir to the throne would be the monarch's blood relative and heir, with no approval or agreement required from the nobility, the military, or the elite citizens. Still, the elective tradition lingered in some places; German and Polish states would retain some form of elective monarchy until the eighteenth century.

Unlike imperial states such as China and Byzantium, and unlike

tant comme il leur pleut. Il les fist convier
et leur donna de ses richesses. Cy fine le
premier livre les historien charlemaine

Cy commence le second livre des histoires char
lemaine, premierement coment il fut cou
ronne a empereur en leglise saint pierre
de romme. Apres coment il condampna
par cil ceulx qui avoient laidi la apostolle
lyon. Et puis des troubles des terres qui
furent par le monde, et des messages et puis
a avoy le roy Sepxze se
e tour de la nativite en
tra lempereur en leglise
saint pierre de romme
droit en ce point que on
avoit celebrer la grant messe. La apostolle

In return for restoring Leo III to the papacy, the pope crowned Charlemagne emperor.

the earlier Roman empire, the early Germanic kingdoms did not think of the state as something that existed in its own right, independent of its individual rulers. The king *was* the only state. His followers swore loyalty to him, not to an impersonal concept of nation or monarchy. Yet a Germanic king did not rule absolutely. Kings were expected to follow tribal laws and customs and to consult with other leaders. They needed the support of the tribe's elite to stay in power. To keep that support, they made compromises, gave favors, and usually ruled by consensus, or general agreement.

## A NEW EUROPEAN EMPIRE

The Franks were a cluster of tribes that settled in what is now France. Their experiment in empire-building would lay the foundation for monarchy throughout much of Europe. It started in the early sixth century with Clovis, the king whose coronation at Rheims came to be linked with the legend of the dove bearing the vial of holy oil from heaven. Clovis became king of all the Franks largely by killing most of his relatives in battle. He then converted to Christianity and brought the Franks into that faith. Having adopted the Roman faith, Clovis tried to adopt also the Roman principle of dynastic or hereditary monarchy. He passed his kingdom to his descendants, who managed to hold onto it for several centuries.

But Clovis's dynastic ambitions were at odds with the Germanic system of inheritance. Like other Germanic peoples, the Franks practiced partible inheritance, which meant that a father's possessions might be inherited by all of his sons. When a king died, his property and the lands he controlled at the time could be divided equally among his heirs. Kingdoms broke up, over time, into smaller and smaller realms. Many royal heirs, however, hungered for more than the shares that fell to them under this system. Wars erupted when brothers fought each other to gain control of the whole Frankish territory. These endless conflicts helped weaken the dynasty that Clovis had founded. By the eighth century, much of the actual power in the Frankish kingdom rested not with the king but with a court official called the mayor of the palace, who governed in the king's name.

In 751 a mayor called Pépin the Short (or Pippin) packed the king off to a monastery and proclaimed himself king. This was no ordinary palace coup. It was an act of deliberate king-making on the part of Pope Zachary, the head of the Roman Catholic Church. The pope had told

Pépin that he would approve the change of power if Pépin would use the Frankish army to defend Rome from its enemies. As a public sign of the church's approval, the pope crowned Pépin in a ceremony that was based on the biblical account of the anointing of King David. This made the ritual of anointing a regular part of the coronation ceremony for European monarchs.

On Pépin's death, each of his two sons inherited half of his kingdom. One son then died, leaving his brother, Charlemagne, the sole king of the Franks. Charlemagne enlarged his kingdom until it included much of present-day Germany and northern Italy. Like his father, he provided much-needed help to the pope of his day, Leo III. In 800, Leo was in trouble—his enemies had not only driven him out of office but had cut out his tongue. Charlemagne brought an army to Rome, restored Leo to the papacy, and received a new title: *imperator augustus,* or emperor, in the style of the old Roman emperors.

Partible inheritance contributed to the downfall of Charlemagne's empire, which was eventually divided among his three grandsons. They and their descendants in turn broke it up still further. Within a couple of centuries, Frankish territory was a patchwork of kingdoms, dukedoms, principalities, and local territories under the rule of castle lords. The title of emperor passed down, however, among the kings of Saxony, in what is now Germany. Although their imperial state was sometimes more an idea than a reality, it included parts of Germany and northern Italy, whose kings were supposed to be subordinate to the emperor. After 1254 this imperial state was known as the Holy Roman Empire. The name emphasized the connection to the imperial state that Charlemagne had created, to the old Roman empire—and to God and the church.

After Pope Leo crowned Charlemagne, becoming a king in Europe was no longer merely a matter of kinship and acclamation. Becoming a king was increasingly seen as a sacrament, a ceremony with divine participation, requiring the involvement of the church. Recognition by the pope legitimized a monarch, making his rule appear rightful and proper, and therefore less likely to be overthrown. As Europe became more fully Christianized, kings came to be seen as God's representatives, governing by divine will. But the relationship between kings and popes was turbulent, swinging back and forth between partnership and conflict. The conflicts were power struggles between monarchs, because the pope was a king, too.

This French print shows Pope Boniface placing the crown on Pépin at his coronation as king in 751. The former mayor became royalty in exchange for his defense of the Roman Catholic Church.

## THE PAPAL MONARCHY

Europeans of the Middle Ages were in a unique situation. "Unlike all other major world civilizations," says W. M. Spellman in *Monarchies: 1000–2000,* medieval Europeans owed allegiance to "two distinct monarchs." One monarch was the king who ruled each particular region. The other was the pope, who was considered the universal monarch over all Christians. The two monarchs needed each other—kings needed popes to legitimize their rule, and popes needed kings to lead the defense of the realm. Yet neither side wanted to submit to the other. The history of medieval Europe was, in part, a struggle between kings and popes over which was the superior authority.

A showdown came in 1076, when Pope Gregory VII challenged Emperor Henry IV. At issue was a power called investiture, which meant appointing people to church positions such as bishop and abbot. Emperors, kings, nobles, and local lords considered these church offices to be, in a sense, their property to distribute as they chose. After all, rulers often gave buildings or even land to religious institutions such as abbeys and bishoprics. The clergy and their priests, clerks, and monks served the monarchs as scribes, tutors, and administrators. Popes, however, felt that the power to hand out offices of the faith lay only with the church. Beneath the question of investiture was a broader question: Would the papal monarchy achieve theocratic power, like that of the Byzantine empire, over *all* western Christians, or would governance remain divided between sacred power (popes) and secular power (kings)?

The eleventh century had brought a reform movement within the church, aimed at tighter control over clergy and greater freedom from political control by outside rulers. First the church claimed the right to have popes elected by high-ranking religious officials called cardinals, not simply chosen by emperors, as had happened in the past. Then Gregory ordered Henry to stop investing bishops. Henry replied by saying that Gregory's claim to the papacy was not legitimate, therefore he need not be obeyed. So Gregory took the most severe action a pope could take. He excommunicated Henry, casting the emperor out of the church. This did more than prevent Henry from going to religious services. It dissolved any allegiance owed to him by members of the church. His nobles and lords were free to choose someone to rule in his place.

With his crown at stake, Henry submitted. He stood barefoot in the snow before the pope and asked for pardon. Gregory granted it—and a few years later Henry marshalled his forces, led an army to Rome, and replaced Gregory with a pope of his own choosing, claiming to be acting only for the good of the church.

The dramatic confrontation between Henry and Gregory did not end the conflict over investiture, which was settled by compromise in the twelfth century. Still, the tug-of-war between popes and kings continued. Early in the fourteenth century the papacy seemed to be losing political power over the kings of Europe. A French writer captured the spirit of the times when he argued that royal rule should have priority over papal rule because it was older. He reminded his readers that "there were kings in France before there were Christians."

Disorder within the church contributed to the decline of papal power. Competing claims by rival popes (once there were three at the same time), corruption among the clergy, and the increasing size and expense of the papal bureaucracy weakened the church's hold on some Europeans. In the early sixteenth century, dissatisfaction with the church led to the Reformation, a movement in which Christians broke from the Roman Catholic Church to establish new Protestant faiths. Yet the influence of the papal monarchy remained strong in Catholic lands, such as Spain and France. And for people in the Papal States, the pope was both a spiritual and temporal, or worldly, monarch.

The Papal States were tracts of land in Italy that were given to the papacy by the Frankish kings and Holy Roman emperors. The first such gift came from Pépin in 754. In time the Papal States came to include the city of Rome and large areas north and east of it, in a band that stretched across the Italian peninsula. Within this territory the pope was both "prince and pastor," as historian Paolo Prodi puts it in *The Papal Prince,* a history of the papal monarchy. During the sixteenth and seventeenth centuries, the power of the papal monarchy was at its height in the Papal States. Eventually, however, the Papal States came under the control of secular rulers. Territory under the sovereign rule of the pope shrank to Vatican City, an enclave within the city of Rome, which the pope still governs as monarch. Centuries before that time, however, the power of Europe's kings started rising. Organized governments began forming under sovereign monarchs, laying the foundations of modern nation-states.

## THE RETURN OF THE KINGS

By the tenth century, Europe had become a lawless, chaotic mess. There were no widespread mechanisms for keeping order. Kings had surprisingly little actual power. They could command armies provided by their loyal followers—but only when those followers considered it in their best interests to obey the king. Much of the countryside was under the direct rule of local lords, nobles, and knights in what has been called the feudal system. Great lords pledged loyalty and service to the king in return for titles and large estates. Lesser lords pledged loyalty to greater lords for a share of those estates. Knights pledged to fight for nobles, who housed and fed the knights. The king was at the top of the feudal system but was often unable to control the powerful lords, whose estates and armies might be larger than the monarch's.

Fighting among feudal lords and their armed followers was so common and so disruptive that the church issued calls for a "Peace of God" or "Truce of God," pleading with knights to halt their violence for certain periods, such as between Wednesday night and Monday morning. The Crusades, a series of wars in which European Christians attacked Muslim-controlled lands in the Middle East, were partly a way for the church and kings to harness the restless energy of the warrior class in a religious cause.

Conditions brightened in the eleventh century. Europe's population began to increase for the first time in centuries. Agriculture and trade improved. Towns and cities grew, and so did a merchant class that wanted an orderly, lawful society in which to do business. The rise of this urban merchant class gave kings a chance to raise some much-needed funds.

European kings did not command all the wealth of their realms. Most of them did not even receive taxes. They had to support themselves, their courts, and their armies—and not all kings were rich. They lived on the income of their estates and whatever else they made in the form of gifts or payments for the favors they granted to followers. To gain power over the semi-independent nobles and warriors, monarchs needed soldiers, and soldiers cost money. Kings began granting the rising towns certain rights and privileges, such as letting them govern their own civic affairs, hold their own courts of justice, and move trade goods freely from place to place, in exchange for fees paid to the crown. Those fees helped pay for military strength that helped enforce the king's law. Townspeople, in turn, acknowledged the king's authority. In a sense, the monarchs and the merchants had made an alliance that offered practical benefits to both sides, while it curbed the power of ambitious, rebellious, or troublesome nobles.

England led the way in the development of a unified nation under centralized royal rule. Once part of the old Roman empire, England was later divided among a cluster of small kingdoms. One of them, Wessex, eventually controlled much of England. Distinctive features of this monarchy included a system of sheriffs and courts for enforcing royal law (and preventing local lords from taking the law into their own hands), a national army (to limit the power of the nobles' private armies), and an assembly called a *witan*, a setting for discussion and debate among the king, lords, judges, high churchmen, and other important figures.

When invaders from the Normandy region of France conquered England in 1066, they kept these useful features of centralized government and added new ones. The Norman rulers outlawed private wars between nobles; they also kept the power of the nobles in check by regulating the building of new castles. One of their first and most significant acts was ordered by William I, the conqueror of England. It was a survey, or inventory, of all landholdings (including livestock) in the realm—and their value. The result, called the Domesday Book, listed all properties in England, with the exceptions of some large cities, including London. Nevertheless, it became the basis for collecting taxes and fees owed to the crown.

The Normans strengthened government institutions such as a national exchequer, or treasury, and royal courts of justice. They replaced what remained of England's inconsistent local laws with a common law for the entire country, and they began allowing jury trials, in which a person's guilt or innocence was decided by fellow citizens instead of by a single judge or royal representative. These measures helped build a shared national identity for the English people, who increasingly saw themselves as subjects of the king, not of the local lords.

Europe's royal governments benefited from a revival in the study of law that started in the eleventh century. Scholarship in both ancient Roman law and church law was a major focus of the new universities that were coming into existence. The idea of a state as being united and governed by a body of laws, rather than by the changing whims of

Threatened with insurrection by his own men, King John reluctantly signed the Magna Carta at Runnymede on June 15, 1215.

rulers, began to take hold. At the same time, legal scholars recognized the right of kings to make laws and collect taxes for the good of the people. Rulers were seen as having both rights and responsibilities, or obligations. Kingship was becoming a balancing act, or negotiation, in which kings had to meet at least some of the needs of various groups—the church, the nobles, and the people—in order to retain their support.

The Magna Carta is the best-known example of that negotiation. In 1215 King John of England signed this document reluctantly, after he was defeated in battle by a force made up of his own nobles, knights, churchmen, and townsmen. The Magna Carta was a list of their demands; the king had no choice but to agree to them. Among other things, the Magna Carta prevented the king from abusing his powers and from eliminating jury trials. It became a symbol of the principle that even the king is not above the law.

## CHALLENGES TO ROYAL POWER

Some scholars see the Magna Carta as the beginning of constitutional monarchy, a kind of kingdom in which rulers are bound by the same constitutions, or sets of laws, as their subjects. Yet the Magna Carta was not written as a rallying cry for a new, more modern type of government. It was mainly about money. The Magna Carta was a protest against the extreme steps King John had taken to pay for wars in France. "In order to raise money for his battles," writes historian Barbara Hanawalt, "he forced the English nobility and townspeople to pay more taxes than they had ever paid before. . . . He insisted on turning a profit from every feudal right that he had over the nobility. For instance, he sold the right to marry noble widows." The Magna Carta corrected these abuses. It let the king impose ordinary taxes, but extra or special taxes had to be approved by the same groups—nobles, knights, churchmen, and townsmen—that had forced him to sign the agreement.

Those groups were careful to protect the rights they had gained under the Magna Carta. When John was succeeded by his young son Henry III, they formed a council, modeled on the witan of Wessex, to rule as his regent. But when Henry came of age and took on full kingship, he fought against the council and its limitations on royal power. A noble named Simon de Montfort led the resistance against the king. To gain support for his side, Montfort invited cities and towns to send more representatives to the council. This was the origin of

Parliament, which included two elected members from each English county and large town.

After Henry's death, his successor Edward I found Parliament useful for notifying the country of royal plans and announcing new taxes. At first, Parliament generally approved the king's requests without question. Before long, however, members of Parliament were questioning, criticizing, and negotiating with the king. They had become directly involved in governing England.

France had a similar parliamentary body called the Estates-General. Parliaments developed in other monarchies as well. Most of these assemblies were originally unelected councils made up of nobles or aristocrats and high-level clergymen. Like England's Parliament, they eventually expanded to include elected representatives from cities, towns, and counties. Parliamentary powers were limited—for example, parliaments met when monarchs summoned them, and monarchs could dismiss them. Yet monarchs needed order and support at home if they wanted to pursue expensive projects, such as the Hundred Years' War between England and France. Working with parliaments helped kings get cooperation from both nobles and ordinary people, and so, over time, parliamentary power became solidly established.

A different challenge to kingly power emerged in Italy in the thirteenth century, at the dawn of the Renaissance. New types of government took shape in the cities of northern Italy. The self-governing communes, or civic associations, of the late Middle Ages shook off the authority of dukes, counts, princes, and bishops and organized themselves into republics that were inspired by the political philosophy of Aristotle and the republican ideals of early Rome. Although power and participation in government were generally limited to the upper classes, and some republics were taken over by strong leaders who became despots, republican governments endured for several centuries in Florence, Genoa, Venice, and smaller cities. As an alternative and a challenge to European monarchies, these republics influenced later political thinkers such as Thomas Paine.

The republic of Florence produced one of the most influential political theorists of the Renaissance. Niccolò Machiavelli served as a member of the city's governing council, responsible for both diplomacy and military defense. His career as a politician ended when, with help from Pope Julius II, the powerful Medici family gained control

NICOL:MACCHIAVELLI

Machiavelli's theories on power—how to get it, how to keep it—remain current more than 500 years after the publication of *The Prince*.

of Florence in 1512 and dissolved the republic. Machiavelli spent the remaining fifteen years of his life writing about politics. His *Discorsi* (*Discourses*) uses the works of the ancient Roman historian Livy as the starting point for a discussion of the structure and strengths of a republican form of government. Far better known, however, is *Il principe* (*The Prince*), first published in 1532, five years after Machiavelli's death.

*The Prince* focuses on "new princes"—rulers who are not members of hereditary dynasties but who rise to power on their own and defend it through military might and strategy. Although Machiavelli states that a prince should act for the good of the state, not for personal power, he also says that to be successful, a ruler must be prepared to act in ways that are ruthless, even at times immoral. With its exploration of the politics of power, *The Prince* functioned almost as a handbook for the monarchs in the sixteenth century and beyond.

# 5
## Divine Right and Revolution ■ ■ ■

AFTER THE COLLAPSE of the old Roman empire, two views of government existed in Western Europe. In the eyes of the church, authority descended from above. It came from God to a monarch who, as God's representative, was the supreme authority on earth. The Germanic tribes, however, saw authority as rising up from the people to their king. The monarch ruled by the people's consent. He could be opposed, or even dethroned, if he abused his power or ruled poorly. These opposing views of monarchic authority—that it came from a divine source and that it came from the people—lingered.

During the seventeenth and eighteenth centuries, political thinkers and writers took a close look at the institution of monarchy. While many of them tried to determine what type of monarchy was best, others daringly questioned whether monarchy was necessary at all. Meanwhile, the fortunes of monarchs swung wildly, from the pinnacle of power to the executioner's scaffold.

### ABSOLUTISM
The Reformation that split the church into Catholic and Protestant versions of Christianity was a religious movement, but it was political, too. On one level, the simple fact of a break within the church raised fears of further disruptions of social order. If even the church could be

The Council of Trent was a response by the Catholic Church to the Reformation. It might have been the last stand for the divine right of kings.

defied, broken apart, and remade, were monarchies safe? The "natural order" of things seemed suddenly subject to change—a prospect that unnerved many people.

On another level, the Reformation contributed to violent conflict. Some countries remained Catholic while others became Protestant, and the suspicion and hostility that each religion felt toward the other fed into national antagonisms. King Henry VIII had withdrawn England from the Catholic Church in the sixteenth century, for example, and after that time English enmity toward Spain and France was magnified by the fact that both were Catholic lands. In Protestant and Catholic countries alike, religious authorities turned to the secular authorities— the monarchs—to enforce the "correct" religion. The results, including massacres of Protestants in France and persecution of Catholics in England, created more civil strife.

In this time of disagreement and disorder, scholars turned to political philosophy for guidance on how nations should be governed. The Renaissance had revived interest in ancient, pre-Christian texts, including Plato's *Republic* and Aristotle's *Politics*; centuries' worth of religious writings had explored issues such as authority and obedience; and the principles of both civil and church law were widely studied. Drawing on these backgrounds, political thinkers developed two main ideas about government. These were the theories of natural law and divine right.

The natural law theory took its inspiration from the ancient world. The Greeks and Romans had viewed human beings as political animals. They had experimented with systems of government and tried to determine the best kind of polity, or state. The ancient philosophy called Stoicism had concluded that human relationships and societies are governed by unchanging principles—laws that are built into the nature of things.

In the seventeenth century, a Dutch legal scholar named Hugo Grotius and an English political philosopher named Thomas Hobbes explored the Stoic concept of natural law. They held that the natural laws of human and social behavior can be discovered by reason, and that these laws should form the basis of political systems. In Hobbes's view, human beings are driven by greedy, violent impulses that can only be controlled by a forceful authority. People in society must yield their liberty to that authority, but in return the ruler protects them. The ruler did not have to be a monarch, according to Hobbes. A dictator or other autocrat would be equally able to provide security and order. The ruler, however, must have undivided power. Without absolute rule, society would fall apart.

Hobbes was critical of religion, but the other theory of kingship that developed in the seventeenth century—the divine right theory— was rooted in religious belief. It drew upon *The City of God,* by St. Augustine, an early Christian thinker. According to Augustine, God created earthly societies and secular rulers to protect the community of believers. Even an ungodly monarch, therefore, ruled through God's authority. To question a monarch's right to rule, or to view political organization as a purely human creation and not a divinely guided one, was to question God's plan for humankind.

A seventeenth-century French bishop and historian named Jacques Bénigne Bossuet was one of several thinkers who developed this idea into what Bossuet called "the divine right of kings." According to Bossuet, kings were appointed by God to rule. And because God's will cannot be divided, a king must rule as an autocrat, with absolute power and authority. If nobles, parliaments, mobs in the street, or even the church rebelled against the king or tried to share power, they were defying God.

Bossuet also argued that the divine right of kings required succession by primogeniture, a system of inheritance that had largely replaced partible inheritance in Europe by the sixteenth century. Where partible inheritance had divided estates among heirs, primogeniture gave the estate to the oldest son. Under primogeniture, a king's oldest son inherited the throne. Although that sounds simple, the rules of primogeniture could be complicated, especially where royal succession was concerned. A set of principles called the order of succession determined who would inherit the throne if there were no oldest son to take it. The order of succession differed from monarchy to monarchy, varying in such matters as whether daughters and their children could inherit, whether brothers inherited before stepsons and nephews inherited before cousins, and the like.

Resistance to primogeniture was common. Nobles and aristocrats did not easily give up the last remnants of the ancient practice of electing, or approving, their kings. Their reasons for wanting a voice in the selection of the king were sometimes selfish—for example, a group of nobles might back a younger son's claim to the throne, or a brother's,

The English philosopher Thomas Hobbes (1588–1679) argued that people's out-of-control desires must be controlled by a powerful authority.

or a nephew's, or even a pretender's, if they thought he would favor them when he became king. In Bossuet's view, though, no exceptions to primogeniture should be allowed. The God-given right to rule could not be spread out among multiple members of a dynasty.

Natural law and the divine right of kings followed different paths to the same conclusion: an absolute ruler who cannot be questioned and does not share power. This kind of monarchy—called absolutism or absolute monarchy—developed in Portugal and Spain, both of which became global empires by claiming overseas territories after the fifteenth century. In 1580, however, Portugal and its territories came under Spanish control. Portuguese power declined, but Spanish power rose.

During the 1590s, under King Philip II, Spain had the largest military force in western Europe. Its American territories were larger than all of Europe combined. At that time Spain had great influence over the Papal States. The Spanish crown had donated vast sums of money to repair old churches and to build new ones in Rome and other papal territories. A Spanish navy cruised the Mediterranean Sea to protect the Papal States from attack by the Ottoman empire. Philip II was "the most powerful monarch of the sixteenth century and the major foreign patron of Rome." Yet although the papacy depended upon Spain's help, Spain also benefited from the relationship. Spain gained influence and prestige as the papal protector, and the example of absolute rule in the Papal States served to reinforce the same kind of rule in Spain. Although its power gradually faded, Spain remained an absolute monarchy until the nineteenth century.

### "I AM THE STATE!"

Thomas Hobbes published *Leviathan*, his best-known work on natural law and politics, in 1651. By that time England had already rejected absolute monarchy—with an executioner's axe. The king of Scotland ascended to the English throne as James I in 1603. Not only was he a Catholic, but he stood before Parliament and talked of the divine right of kings. The speech was not well received. His heir, Charles I, also asserted his divine right to rule, and he suspended Parliament.

Civil war broke out in the early 1640s between Royalists (including many Catholics) and Parliamentarians (led by Protestant Puritans). When the Parliamentarians won, they beheaded the king, an act

William and Mary ruled jointly as king and queen of England, but with their ascension to the throne, real power moved to Parliament. This painting by Anthony van Dyck, shows them as children.

known as regicide, or king-killing. They next established a republican government called the Commonwealth, with Oliver Cromwell as protector, or head of state. Conditions in the Commonwealth were unsettled, with tension between civilian and military leaders and no clear plan for the role of Parliament, at the time of Cromwell's death in 1658.

Cromwell's son succeeded him as protector but lacked his father's ability to inspire loyalty. He failed to rally popular support or manage Parliament or the army. With the country on the brink of chaos, Parliament invited the executed king's heir, Charles II, to return from exile and take the throne in 1660. Charles II died in 1685, but not before managing to pass the succession to his brother, James II. The new king refused to compromise with Parliament on important issues, took the unpopular step of advancing many Catholics to prominent positions, and, above all, seemed to believe that he had a divine right to rule. James had been on the throne only three years when a group of England's religious and political leaders asked his Protestant son-in-law, William of Orange, to take over as king. James fled to France, leaving the monarchy in the hands of his daughter Mary and her husband, who ruled jointly.

England's Glorious Revolution, as the arrival of William and Mary was called, placed power firmly in the hands of Parliament. The new monarchs agreed to a Bill of Rights that ensured regular parliamentary sessions and free elections. Monarchs, it was now understood, did not rule by divine right—at least, not in England. They ruled by the consent of Parliament. In 1701 a law called the Act of Settlement shifted the responsibility for sovereign activities from the monarch to the ministers of state. Soon monarchs no longer attended Parliament, and the responsibility for heading the government fell to the new office of the prime minister. Then, in 1832, the Reform Act stated that sovereignty lay not with the monarch but with the people and their representatives in Parliament. The British monarchy had become more or less what it is today—a traditional, ceremonial position.

France's absolute monarch was Bossuet's own king, Louis XIV, who reigned from 1643 to 1715. Louis retained tight personal control over all aspects of governing the realm; he shared power only with a small group of trusted ministers and refused to summon a meeting of the Estates-General throughout his entire reign. The king's confidence in his power and his right to rule shows in his most famous statement: *"L'état c'est moi"* ("I am the state"). Louis's control, however, came at great cost. He ordered his powerful nobles, the ones who might have challenged his absolutism, to become full-time courtiers so that he could keep them under his eye and under control. In return, he relieved them from paying royal taxes. Louis also freed the church from royal taxation so that it would support him without question.

As a result of Louis's tax breaks for the aristocrats and the church, the crown's income dropped drastically—but Louis needed money to support his lavish court, where a constant round of ceremonies, parties, and royal audiences followed elaborate rules of etiquette that emphasized the king's superiority over everyone else. So Louis sought to fill his treasury from the only source left: the French commoners and peasants. They were taxed more heavily than ever before, which created growing misery and resentment. By the time Louis died, the crown was bankrupt, and the population of overtaxed working poor people had become a time bomb.

## NEW LIGHT ON PEOPLE AND MONARCHS

A quarter of a century before the death of Louis XIV, an English scholar and political thinker named John Locke published a book called *Two Treatises of Government*. Like Hobbes's *Leviathan*, *Two Treatises* started from the idea that human beings come together in societies for safer, better lives than they would have if each remained on his or her own, in a state of nature. Locke, however, had a more benign view of human nature than Hobbes. People, Locke thought, are essentially reasonable beings.

Locke believed in natural law, too. In his view, natural law says that all people are entitled to life, freedom, and ownership of property. They form associations, or governments, to protect those rights. But a government is a contract, similar to a legal contract: If one party breaks it, the other party is no longer bound by it. To Locke, this meant that if a government ceases to rule fairly and to protect the people's natural rights, the people are free to reject their government.

During the eighteenth century, Locke's ideas became one of many strands woven into an intellectual movement known as the Enlightenment. Although the Enlightenment was centered in France, in the writings of philosophers such as Voltaire and Jean-Jacques

Rousseau, it also involved Swiss, German, Italian, and Scottish thinkers. In general, the Enlightenment celebrated the power of reason to solve social problems and improve human lives. Applied to politics, the Enlightenment carried on Hobbes's and Locke's concern with the relationship between individuals and the state, and with the proper nature of government. Concepts such as civil liberties appear often in Enlightenment writings, although Enlightenment thinkers did not share a single vision of what government should be.

Some Enlightenment philosophers, including Voltaire, believed that the best form of government was an "enlightened absolutism" or "enlightened despotism." In such a government, all power would rest with a single ruler who would be guided by a rational belief in natural law and a desire to promote universal well-being. This type of state did come into existence in a few places during the eighteenth century. Rulers such as Frederick I of Prussia and Catherine the Great of Russia governed with absolute power yet wanted to reform their societies according to Enlightenment principles. Their efforts were limited by the fact that they refused to give up any power, and although their successors were despots, they were not very enlightened.

Other Enlightenment thinkers tended toward republican, representative government. English political theorists John Trenchard and Thomas Gordon in *Cato's Letters or Essays on Liberty, Civil and Religious, and Other Important Subjects*, argued against the divine right of kings and claimed that governments are accountable to their subjects. These writers and Locke influenced the thinking of American colonists such as John Adams, Thomas Jefferson, and Thomas Paine, who helped ignite the American Revolution against British rule in the 1770s.

The American Revolution was a milestone in the history of monarchy. A territory had cast off the rule of the crown that had claimed it and colonized it. Even more significant, the newly independent territory had established a new form of government: a democratic republic. The example of the American Revolution would inspire other populations to rebel against monarchs and to experiment with systems of government.

Yet the American Revolution was not originally intended as a complete break with tradition—or even a complete break with Britain. At first, the dissatisfied colonists who became the patriots and the Founding Fathers merely wanted to correct an injustice. They were being ruled by the British Parliament yet were not allowed to send voting representatives to Parliament. If they had been given a voice in the British government when they first demanded it, the Revolution might not have happened. Even when it did happen, a large number of colonists were passionately against it.

Only when it became clear that the break with Britain was unavoidable did some of the colonists begin thinking about the new government they would create in America. And although they chose republicanism, some among them wanted the United States to have a king. A few people even approached George Washington, who had led the American military through the Revolution, and asked if he would be interested in becoming king. He refused, and the office of the president took on the functions of both head of government and head of state of the United States. But although the American Revolution is commonly spoken of as the colonists' revolt against King George III of Great Britain, and although the Declaration of Independence lists their grievances against the king, it was really Parliament against whom they rebelled. By the time of the American Revolution, the British monarchy had lost most of its former power. The French monarchy was still an absolute monarchy, at least in name, but that was about to change.

The American colonists won the Revolution with help from France, which had supported the revolt mainly to spite and weaken its longtime rival Great Britain. Meanwhile, however, France's internal politics were becoming explosive. For the great mass of ordinary French people, conditions under King Louis XVI were as bad as they had been under Louis XIV, or worse. Six years after the American Revolution ended in 1783, rebellion reared its head in the streets of Paris, and the French Revolution was under way. Four years after that, in 1793, the king and Queen Marie Antoinette joined the other victims of the Revolution who lost their heads to the guillotine.

Unlike the American Revolution, the French Revolution did not succeed in establishing a stable, long-lasting republic. It ushered in an unstable period that has been called the Reign of Terror. Revolutionary leaders struggled to define a new government while wiping out nobles, aristocrats, and other traces of the old regime. In a powerfully symbolic act of antimonarchism, revolutionaries went to the cathedral in Rheims and destroyed the vial from which French kings had been anointed since medieval times.

For all its determination to destroy the monarchy, the French Revolution gave birth to a new imperial state in Europe. A successful military commander named Napoleon Bonaparte ascended to the position of first consul, the highest office of France's new republic, and then, in 1804, at the height of his popularity, made himself emperor with the support of the people.

The Revolution had been carried out in the name of bringing liberty, brotherhood, and equality to the people of France. At first some political thinkers in France and other countries saw it as the rebirth of a nation. Napoleon's interests, however, lay outside France's borders. He embarked on a campaign to dominate Europe through military conquest, and by 1810 he had achieved much success. Napoleon claimed to be spreading the ideals of the French Revolution to other countries so that Europe could be united under a single government run on Enlightenment principles. In reality, as he overthrew existing monarchs, he replaced them with his own relatives. The legal and economic reforms Napoleon introduced in the countries he conquered did not make the people of those countries love him; resistance remained strong, and opposition from Britain was ceaseless.

The Battle of Waterloo in 1815 brought Napoleon's empire to its final end. The battle also marks the end of the social and political experiment that was the French Revolution. Afterward, the European powers met in Vienna, Austria, to create a peace settlement that would end the Napoleonic Wars. Led by Prince Klemens von Metternich of Austria, the assembled powers agreed that respect for monarchy and aristocracy must be restored to Europe, and that monarchy was the only suitable form of government. In France, Spain, Sicily, and various small kingdoms in Italy, surviving heirs to the former monarchies were placed on thrones. Yet these restored monarchies were different from the absolute monarchies that had existed before Napoleon. Monarchs now accepted constitutions that curbed their power. Legislatures were responsible for making laws and imposing taxes. Parliaments and other assemblies took on greater roles in government and overseeing royal behavior. The French Revolution had not eliminated monarchy, but it had certainly limited it.

The return to monarchy that Metternich had crafted failed to satisfy millions of Europeans. Workers and the middle class remained unhappy with the fact that they had little or no political power. In France, a second revolution in 1848 overthrew the new monarchy and

Napoleon Bonaparte started on the side of the Revolution and ended as an exiled emperor. At his coronation, Napolean took the crown and placed it on his own head.

# Metaphors for Monarchy

What is the true nature of monarchy? What is the king's proper relationship to his subjects? For centuries, people have answered these questions with metaphors, comparisons in the form of images. The two most enduring metaphors for monarchy were the family and the body. They brought the abstract concept of monarchy down to the level of universal human experience: Everyone knows what a family is, and everyone has a body. But the metaphors also served to support the institution of monarchy by making it seem natural, even inevitable—just like family life and physical existence.

The comparison of the state to the family appears in the writings of several ancient civilizations. In China, people believed that a family is a hierarchical structure, one organized into ranks or levels of power, with a recognized place for everyone and all authority concentrated at the top, in the father. This vision of proper family structure harmonized with a hierarchical state, in which power and authority were concentrated in the king, and later in the emperor. Confucianism, China's widely shared system of ethical principles, reinforced that connection. It specifically compared a well-run state to the family and a well-run family to the state.

The ancient Greeks also drew upon the state-as-family metaphor. When asked why he had not established a democracy in Sparta, the lawmaker Lycurgus is said to have replied, with irony, "Begin, friend, and set one up in your own family." Aristotle used the metaphor in Book I of his *Politics*, saying that "the government of a household is a monarchy, since every house is governed by a single ruler." Later in the same book, however, Aristotle pointed out the weaknesses of the metaphor: "Some thinkers . . . suppose that statesman, king, estate manager, and master of a family have a common character." This, Aristotle argued, was a mistake.

Still, the metaphor of the monarchy as a family, with the king as the authoritarian but protective father, was useful to political writers as long as family structures remained hierarchical and patriarchal, or dominated by fathers. In many parts of the world today, however, the strongly patriarchal family is no longer the norm. Still, writers and speechmakers continue to use the state-as-family metaphor, although they don't mention parental monarchs. They are more likely to employ the metaphor in general terms, perhaps calling the population of the United States "our American family" or referring to "the family of nations."

The other long-lasting metaphor for the state is the body. Not only is a state or population united under a government sometimes called "the body politic," but the metaphor underlies such phrases as "the head of state" or "an arm of the government." When the body metaphor is applied to monarchy, the monarch is the head, the seat of decision making and will.

In 1159 an English churchman named John of Salisbury came up with the body metaphor in an attempt to resolve the long conflict between the church and monarchs over who had ultimate authority. John compared a people or state to "a sort of body." Its soul was the church. Its head was the prince, or king. Four centuries later, an English law reflected the belief that the people should obey their monarch as the body obeys the will of the head, or mind. Written in 1532 or 1533, during the reign of King Henry VIII, the law states: "This Realm of England is an Empire . . . governed by one supreme Head and King . . . unto whom a Body politick, compact of all Sorts and Degrees of People . . . been bounden and owen to bear a natural and humble Obedience . . ."

The king-as-head metaphor is gruesomely appropriate for societies that rid themselves of their monarchs—and their monarchies—through decapitation. Most regicides have simply ushered in the reigns of new kings. But the beheadings of King Charles I of England in 1649 and of Louis XVI of France in 1793 marked the end of monarchic rule in their countries, at least for a while. Metaphorically *and* literally, the English and French had lopped off their heads of state. Perhaps William Shakespeare had just such perils of kingship in mind when he wrote, in Act III, Scene 1, of *Henry IV, Part II,* "Uneasy lies the head that wears a crown."

established a second republic, which fell three years later to a second empire headed by Napoleon's nephew. That regime remained in power until 1870; it collapsed during a war with Prussia when a German army invaded France. In the aftermath of that war, monarchy almost returned to France, but the representatives who met to form a new government could not agree on which royal claimant to support. In the end, France adopted a presidential system. The French monarchy had again come to an end, this one seemingly final.

In victorious Prussia, by contrast, a new monarchy formed as the princes, dukes, and kings of many German states accepted Wilhelm I, king of Prussia, as their emperor (called *kaiser*, the German version of the ancient *caesar*). This federation brought the modern, united state of Germany into existence. A new monarchy also emerged in Italy, united for the first time under a single king in 1861.

In Austria, the Habsburg dynasty continued to rule over what remained of the old Holy Roman Empire. During the late nineteenth century, however, Emperor Francis Joseph of Austria had to give in to many demands. He gave Hungary, long part of the empire, a considerable amount of self-government; he allowed the formation of representative assemblies and an elected parliament; and he granted his subjects civil rights such as freedom of religion and equal standing under the law. These changes reflected the influence of nationalism, a force that had gained strength across Europe during the Napoleonic Wars.

Nationalism was the strong desire for one's nation to be powerful, successful, and above all independent, not subject to a foreign ruler or dynasty. Nationalism also focused people's loyalties on their nation, not on local or regional identities, individual rulers, or traditional systems of government. One aspect of nationalism, the eagerness of the people to be involved in their governments, led to the liberalization or loosening of monarchic rule in a number of countries.

In Japan, however, nationalism helped restore some authority to the position of the emperor. For hundreds of years, while shoguns of the Tokugawa dynasty governed Japan, the emperors had been mere figureheads, revered but powerless. In the mid-nineteenth century, the warrior and urban commercial classes of Japan began calling for modernization so that Japan would not be economically and politically dominated by other nations, such as the United States. The shoguns turned a deaf ear to these nationalistic demands.

When a new young emperor, Mutsushito, came to the throne in 1867, the leaders of several noble clans turned over their estates and private armies to him in the hope that strengthened imperial authority would move Japan forward. Mutsushito ordered other aristocrats to do the same. He overthrew the Tokugawa shogunate and launched Japan into a period of modernization and reform called the Meiji (Enlightened Rule) Era. The new government that emerged in Japan was a parliament, and although strict rules limited voting to a tiny fraction of the country's population, it was technically a representative government. The emperor did not rule the country directly, any more than he had under the shogunate, but he did control the military and the most important ministers of state.

Some monarchies evolved to meet the demands of revolution or rising nationalism. Others simply ended. In the Americas, European-style monarchies had appeared in only two places: Mexico and Brazil. A Mexican revolutionary leader named Agustin de Iturbide had proclaimed himself emperor in 1822, but without the support of either the army or the people he could not make the claim stick. He was executed a few years later. The French established another empire in Mexico in 1864, placing a European archduke on the throne; he held it for just three years. To the south, in Brazil, the royal family of Portugal—which had fled their country during the Napoleonic Wars—established a dynasty that ruled independent Brazil from 1822 until the Brazilian people's demand for republican government could no longer be ignored. The last king in the Americas left Brazil for Europe in 1889. Two years later, American businessmen in Hawaii overthrew the last native monarch there, Queen Lili'uokalani, paving the way for the United States to claim the Hawaiian islands as U.S. territory in 1898.

At the end of the nineteenth century, although a few new monarchies had formed in Europe, others had ended. Revolution and republicanism had sent shock waves through many lands where royal dynasties still remained in power, such as the Russian empire. Even the ancient empire of China was feeling the pressure of changes in the political climate of the world. The institution of monarchy would soon suffer a blow even more crippling than the French Revolution.

# 6

■ ■■■ Monarchy in the Modern World

IF THE NINETEENTH CENTURY was a difficult time for the institution of monarchy, the twentieth century was a disaster. In 1900, according to historian R. F. Tapsell, nearly 90 percent of the people in the world lived under the rule of some kind of monarch. By 1983, when Tapsell completed his survey of world monarchies, less than one percent did. The world's largest empires, and many smaller monarchies, had collapsed because of the internal pressures of people demanding change, the external pressures of two world wars, or both. And while some monarchies survived, and a handful of new ones were created, the twentieth century saw the end of monarchy as a dominant form of government.

## THE FALL OF EMPIRES

At the beginning of the twentieth century, monarchy ruled the world, in spite of important exceptions such as the Americas and France. A third of the earth's land mass was controlled by just two imperial states: the British and Russian empires. A third empire, China, was the world's most populous country. Monarchy did not mean the same thing in all monarchic states, however. Russia, China, and the Ottoman empire were absolutist states in which the monarchs still wielded supreme authority. At the other extreme, Britain was a

The Chinese empire was the first to fall. Faced with continual rebellions, Empress Cixi made some reforms before her death in 1905, but not enough to stem the antimonarchical tide.

constitutional monarchy in which the monarch had almost no political power. Most European monarchies had constitutions or some kind of representative government that limited the power of their monarchs in varying degrees.

Change came first to China. Since the late eighteenth century, the ancient empire had been torn by a series of revolts in which oppressed, landless, and desperately poor peasants rose up against landlords and tax collectors. The Taiping Rebellion of the mid-nineteenth century, a civil war that raged for years and killed twenty million people or more, shook imperial control because China's rulers had to ask for military help from the United States and Europe to end the rebellion. Militarily and economically weakened, China suffered further disorder after the emperor Tongzhi died without a son in 1875. His mother, the dowager empress Cixi, arranged for her young nephew Guangxu to be named the next emperor; she served as his regent until he came of age. As emperor, Guangxu tried to introduce Western-style reforms to Chinese education and industry. Cixi, fearful of a loss of imperial power, quickly had him arrested and returned to control as regent.

After more rebellions against the crown, Cixi scrambled to make some of the social, political, and economic reforms Guangxu had wanted to make. Before her death in 1905, she eliminated the imperial examination system that had controlled China's civil service bureaucracy for several thousand years. She even offered to introduce constitutional monarchy to China. These offers came too late to halt the demands for change that were increasingly insistent, led mostly by Western-educated students. In 1912, a coup d'état forced the reigning emperor, a six-year-old boy named Puyi, to give up the throne in favor of a republic. In the years to come, China's political organization would be reshaped again and again by civil war and communist revolution, but its long history as a monarchy was over.

But the British and European monarchies, having come through the turbulence of the nineteenth century, appeared secure. Citizens loved the pageantry and symbolism of royalty as much as ever— perhaps more so, now that people felt that they accepted their kings and queens by choice and tradition, not by force. A network of royal relationships seemed to unite England and all of Europe; ties of kinship and marriage linked the rulers of Great Britain, Germany, and Russia, as well as many other royal houses. In 1908, when the Habsburg emperor Francis Joseph reached his sixtieth year on the throne, the dynasties of Europe gathered in Vienna to celebrate. Photographs of this event seem to show one big happy royal family.

Six years later, World War I plunged the continent into war. The main combatants were Britain, France, Russia, Serbia, Italy, and later the United States against Austria, Germany, and the Ottoman empire. In terms of monarchic history, the war was a struggle of ideas "between authoritarianism and dynasticism on the one side and democracy and constitutionalism on the other," according to historian W. M. Spellman. And although Russia was an authoritarian, dynastic empire, that empire collapsed in 1917, in the midst of the war, toppled by revolutionaries who wanted to establish a republic based on the economic principles of communism.

The Russian empire was not the last to fall. When World War I ended in 1918, twenty million people had died. Several imperial regimes also perished. The Austrian empire came to an end, replaced by a republic. Germany lost not just the imperial title of the kaiser but also the twenty-two lesser monarchies in the German federation of states. The Ottoman empire survived in Turkey, but it was stripped of much of its former territory and fatally weakened. In 1920, Turkish nationalists led by a popular military officer named Kemal Ataturk elected a parliament. Two years later they did away with the office of the sultan and established the nation of Turkey, bringing the Ottoman empire to its close.

The monarchies that fared best in the aftermath of World War I were those that had already turned most or all true political power over to representative governments. In addition to Great Britain, these included Norway, Sweden, Denmark, The Netherlands, Belgium, Spain, and Luxembourg (called a grand duchy rather than a monarchy because its dynastic ruler is a grand duke, not a king). All of these constitutional monarchies survived the twentieth century and remain in existence in the early twenty-first century, although Spain's monarchy was abolished in 1931 and restored in 1975.

Other monarchies, however, passed out of existence during or immediately after World War II, which ended in 1945. When the Soviet Union, the communist state that had come to power in Russia, took control of the Eastern European nations of Yugoslavia, Bulgaria, and Romania, for example, it did away with their monarchies. In 1946 the people of Italy voted to end their monarchy.

Japan paid a heavy price for losing World War II. At first, the terms of Emperor Hirohito's surrender included the end of the empire and the establishment of an American-style democracy. But Douglas MacArthur, a general who had commanded U.S. forces in the Pacific and was charged with overseeing the reconstruction of Japan, felt that the emperor was a vitally important national symbol for the Japanese people at this low point in their country's fortunes. If the United States did away with Japan's imperial office, MacArthur claimed, it would create resentment that would "unquestionably last for all measurable time." The emperor therefore remained in office, although he had already voluntarily given up any claim to divine or sacred status. Like the British monarch, the Japanese emperor had become a ceremonial national symbol. Japan's imperial dynasty—the oldest continuous dynasty in the world—still occupies the throne today.

In the second half of the twentieth century, the rising tide of nationalism spawned independence movements in parts of Africa and Asia that were still controlled by foreign colonial powers, such as Great Britain and France. The colonial powers had left many traditional monarchies in place, although the rulers had little power and were sometimes mere puppets. But as these territories gained their independence, sometimes through violence, the new nationalist leaders eliminated many of the traditional monarchies. Various traditional kingdoms within India and Pakistan ended in the 1940s and 1950s, as India and Pakistan became independent British colonial rule. Through revolution, coup, or peaceful decision making, monarchies were also abolished in Egypt, Tunisia, South Africa, Yemen, Afghanistan, Iran, Ethiopia, Laos, Fiji, and other countries.

Yet a few new monarchies were created, mostly in parts of the Muslim world that had formerly belonged to the Ottoman empire. In Syria, Iraq, Egypt, and Jordan, monarchies were established and kings placed on thrones through the support or manipulation of foreign powers, chiefly Britain and France. Saudi Arabia's monarchy emerged with no European involvement. A powerful clan chieftain named Abdul-Aziz ibn Saud proclaimed a kingdom there in 1932; his descendants rule Saudi Arabia today.

## THE FUTURE OF MONARCHY

By far the largest network of monarchies today is linked to the United Kingdom, over which Elizabeth II became queen on that June day in

Not all monarchies have gone the way of the hula hoop. The Saudi government is still ruled by kings. In 1999, King Faud met with then U.S. Secretary of State Madeleine Albright at his palace in Riyadh to discuss affairs of state.

# A Kingdom in Crisis

Nestled beneath the soaring peaks of the Himalayas, the Asian kingdom of Nepal became a top tourist destination in the second half of the twentieth century. People came from all over the world to explore the markets and temples of the capital city of Kathmandu, to trek through spectacular mountain scenery to remote monasteries, and to climb Mt. Everest. But tourism, like much else in Nepal, has changed since June 1, 2001, when monarchic mass murder plunged the country into chaos.

Nepal's royal family was gathered at Narahiti Palace in Kathmandu, residence of King Birendra. Details about that fateful night are not completely clear, but the survivors agree that Crown Prince Dipendra, the king's son and heir, left the rooms in which the family had gathered for drinks before dinner. A short while later he returned, dressed in military fatigues and carrying two assault rifles. He walked up to his father and shot him without a word.

The prince then rushed out into a garden. His mother and younger brother went after him; their bodies were later found in the garden. Less than a minute later, Dipendra returned and killed or wounded more of his relatives. Once more he left the room, only to return almost immediately, again shooting. Then he left and didn't return. He was found in the garden, unconscious, with a gunshot wound.

Dipendra was pronounced king, even though he was in a coma, and even though he had been accused of killing nine of his royal relatives. His own wound, apparently a suicide attempt, was a serious one. He died two days later without regaining consciousness. The Nepali people, meanwhile, were stunned and horrified by news of the massacre, which left ten members of the royal family, including Dipendra, dead. As they groped for a reason for Dipendra's slaughter, stories spread: The prince was drunk, or on drugs, or he wished to marry a woman his parents rejected. At the same time, some Nepalis were suspicous. In a single night, the king, queen, and both princes had died by violence. The line of direct succession to the throne was completely erased, and kingship passed to another branch of the royal family. Gyanendra, an uncle of the murderous prince, became king. His son Paras had been one of the survivors of the fatal night.

The bloody royal shake-up came at a time of political turmoil and uncertainty in Nepal. Traditionally, the Nepalese people have revered their monarchs. Even in recent times, some regarded the kings worshipfully, almost as though they were gods in the Hindu religion that most of the people follow. At the same time, however, modernization, education, and increased contact with the rest of the world have given many Nepalis a desire for self-government.

In response to pressure for change and democratization, in 1990 King Birendra gave up much of the monarchy's power to a democratic government made up of many political parties. Yet Nepal did not move smoothly into its new era. Conflict among rival political parties made it hard to form and maintain governing coalitions. Between 1990 and 2001, Nepal had ten different governments. Many citizens felt that the experiment with democracy was not going well because the parties were corrupt and incapable of good government.

Rural areas also began suffering outbreaks of violence by Maoist rebels, who take inspiration from a version of communism imposed in China in the twentieth century by Mao Zedong. Armed with guns and small, homemade bombs, the Maoists terrorized whole regions, forcing young people to join them and demanding cash payments from peasants, businesses, schools, and tourists. Armed conflicts between local people and Maoist groups, and between Maoists and the police and military, brought death and simmering civil disorder to areas outside the capital. Nepal's tourism income dropped when word spread that trekking in the country's mountains could end in an encounter with armed Maoists.

If Nepal was politically unstable before Prince Dipendra opened fire on his family, the royal massacre made things even worse. The new monarch, King Gyanendra, sought to reclaim some of the former royal power. In October 2002 he dismissed the elected government and appointed a new government in its place. A series of other appointed governments followed. On February 1, 2005, Gyanendra went further. He carried out what one international journal called "a well-executed coup against his own government." Declaring a state of national emergency, Gyanendra claimed absolute power for the monarchy.

The king arrested the prime minister and other political leaders who might have opposed him (most were soon released). Under his command, the army took control of newspaper offices and television studios to censor the news. Telephone service was suspended. Police and the army kept protests to a minimum, but many of the Nepalis who did take to the streets in protests were arrested. Some accounts say that they were tortured.

King Gyanendra of Nepal is shown in royal state with the Princess Purnika. In 2005, Gyanendra gave himself absolute monarchical power.

The king claimed that with power once again in the hands of the monarchy, he would be free to make effective use of the army and halt the Maoist uprising. For this reason, many business leaders in Nepal approved of the royal coup. They hoped that it would restore order. But that didn't happen. Instead, violence between troops and Maoists increased. By the spring of 2006, after about a decade of Maoist rebellion, the death toll had risen to nearly 13,000. At that time the leaders of seven of Nepal's political parties formed an alliance with some Maoist leaders in opposition to the king's seizure of power. Demonstrations against the king broke out in the streets of Kathmandu; the police and the military responded with force. In April 2006, recognizing that he needed to win the support of the people, King Gyanendra offered to let the opposition leaders nominate a prime minister and form a new government. They rejected the offer because the king had not agreed to their chief demands: a parliament and a constitution.

Will absolute monarchy endure in Nepal? Most outsiders think that is unlikely, because the king has proved unable to stop the civil violence or control the Maoists. Nepal is poor and underdeveloped. It needs substantial foreign aid to survive, and prolonged civil war would threaten that aid. The United Nations, India, Great Britain, the United States, and various European nations have spoken of the need for a compromise between the king and the opposition leaders. But how much will the king be willing to yield? Many Nepalis who oppose the king want to see him give up nearly all power and become a ceremonial figurehead. A few want to eliminate the monarchy altogether. King Gyanendra, the twelfth monarch in a dynasty that has ruled Nepal since the eighteenth century, is not likely to welcome either of those prospects. Like many other, larger countries before it, Nepal is experiencing the clash of an old monarchy with the new demands of a changing world.

1953. A number of Britain's former colonies, now independent nations, have chosen to remain linked to the United Kingdom in a loose association of more than fifty states called the British Commonwealth of Nations. Fifteen of the Commonwealth nations have kept the king or queen of the United Kingdom as their official head of state, although all fifteen are self-governing. As a result of this arrangement, the British monarch is also the official head of state of Australia, Canada, and a host of smaller Commonwealth states around the globe, from Antigua and Barbuda in the Caribbean to Tuvalu in the Pacific.

Some other existing monarchies are quite small. These include Vatican City, with the pope as monarch; the Mediterranean princedom of Monaco; and the constitutional principality of Andorra, in the Pyrenees Mountains between France and Spain, which has a unique dual monarchy. Andorra's co-monarchs are the bishop of Seu d'Urgell, in Spain, and the president of France. Between these two extremes are national monarchies such as those of Thailand, Morocco, Lesotho in southern Africa, Spain, and the Scandinavian countries. Malaysia has an elective monarchy in which the king, chosen from among the hereditary rulers of nine traditional states, rules for five years. In addition, kingship has survived or been introduced in a number of places that are not nations but rather traditional regions within nations. In 1993, for example, the government of the African nation of Uganda restored five traditional monarchies within its borders. Although they have little political power on the national level, these monarchies do wield some influence in local and regional administration, but their role is mainly ceremonial. Zululand, a region inside South Africa, also has a traditional king, and the Maori people of New Zealand recognize a king or queen who is not recognized in the nation's constitution but has ceremonial functions.

Saudi Arabia is one of the few kingdoms in today's world governed by an absolute monarch rather than a constitutional one. Bhutan, Brunei, Oman, and Qatar are also absolute monarchies or sultanates, although their rulers find it necessary to keep the military, business, and religious powers within their realms satisfied, just as medieval monarchs had to balance the interests of the nobles, townsmen, and church to stay in power. Other Islamic kingdoms, including Bahrain, Jordan, Kuwait, and Morocco, are considered semiconstitutional monarchies because, even though these countries have constitutions, their rulers retain a fair degree of power. In other modern monarchies, though, government is entirely constitutional. Legislatures make the laws, and elected officials run the government. So what role does a monarch play in today's world?

The typical answer is that a monarch is a symbol of national unity and tradition, a morale-builder for the people, and a piece of living history. Certainly that is often true. Very many people do feel pride in their "royals" and attachment to them. Events such as the birth of a daughter to Crown Prince Naruhito and Princess Masako of Japan in 2001, or Queen Elizabeth's fiftieth anniversary on the British throne in 2003, can inspire great public excitement in a country.

The excitement is not always confined to the country in question. The BBC telecast of Elizabeth's coronation in 1953 showed that people around the world are interested in the pageantry and splendor of royal occasions. When Elizabeth's son Charles married a young Englishwoman named Diana Spencer in 1981, millions watched the ceremony on television. People in many countries avidly followed stories of the "fairytale" marriage, its slow and dismal failure, and the 1996 divorce of Charles and Diana. The princess's death in a car crash in 1997 sparked a public display of grief that extended far beyond the British Commonwealth and even inspired the movie, *The Queen*.

In a culture of celebrity, royals are celebrities with crowns. Their deeds—and especially their misdeeds, mistakes, and scandals—are broadcast to the world on magazine covers and the front pages of tabloid newspapers. Monarchs have become a form of entertainment, giving rise to the term *royal watcher*.

Headline-grabbing royal misbehavior may make citizens question whether the monarchy is worth its cost. In Norway in 2001, after a series of articles criticizing the romantic lives of Prince Haakon and Princess Martha Louise, support for the monarchy fell to just 59 percent of the population, down from 71 percent a year earlier. Such criticisms occur in more serious contexts, too. From time to time in many monarchies—at least the constitutional ones—newspaper articles or political speeches raise the question of whether the monarchy is useful in any way, is too expensive to maintain, or is a fading relic of a bygone era. Monarchs who are extremely wealthy, such as the sultan of Brunei, the queen of England, and the prince of Liechtenstein, are sometimes seen as hoarders of personal wealth that could better be used to help a greater number of people. The British royals and others have worked hard to take the edge off such criticisms through such means as volunteering to pay income tax like ordinary citizens and becoming visibly involved in worthy activities for charities or the environment.

A few monarchs are returning to political life, sometimes in nontraditional ways. Norodom Sihanouk of Cambodia, for example, has held an array of political positions, including king, prince, president, and prime minister. Another versatile monarch is Simeon II, Bulgaria's last tsar. He came to the throne in 1943, when he was six years old, and lost it three years later when the country's new communist government abolished the monarchy. Simeon grew up in exile in Spain, but in 1996, after communism was overturned in Bulgaria, he returned to his homeland and was greeted by cheering mobs. He formed a new political party, was elected to the national parliament, and served as prime minister from 2001 to 2005. Prince Hans-Adam II of Liechtenstein, a small principality sandwiched between Switzerland and Austria, flexed his political muscles in 2003, threatening to move to Austria with his family if the constitutional government tried to reduce his powers. The government confirmed his powers. Although Liechtenstein is tiny, hardly an important player in world affairs, its sovereign has more political clout than is the case in most larger constitutional monarchies.

With the appeal of history and tradition, royals are often more popular than the people who actually run a country. And if they returned to power, they might do a better job than some incompetent and corrupt governments. Yet a large-scale return of monarchy is unlikely, even though there are enthusiastic groups, in many countries and on the Internet, devoted to restoring out-of-work monarchs to their thrones, or even to establishing new monarchies.

Some political theorists have put forward the case for monarchy as well. In 2001, for example, political philosopher Robert Kraynak published *Christian Faith and Modern Democracy: God and Politics in the Fallen World,* an attempt to revive St. Augustine's concept of a hierarchical society on earth as a mirror of the divine kingdom of God. Kraynak argued that people have lost their way under democracy, which does nothing to ensure their spiritual well-being. He outlined a model government with features drawn from monarchy, aristocracy, and republicanism, yet said nothing about how such a form of government might affect people who did not share its Christian underpinnings.

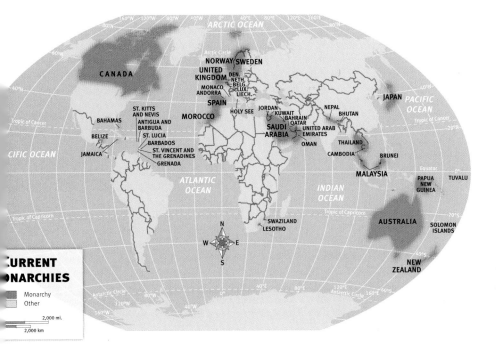

**Monarchies in the World Today**

Despite the fans of royal pageantry and the philosophers who see merit in monarchy, the institution of kingship seems out of step with the modern world. Many people today believe that the proper relationship of people to one another should be egalitarian, or equal, not hierarchical. But the tide of history has shifted before, and monarchy, which is as old as civilization, is extremely adaptable. It has survived in many forms over the centuries. The rule of the monarch may not make a comeback, but it is unlikely to disappear.

# Monarchy and Other Governments

| MONARCHY* | COMMUNISM | SOCIALISM |
|---|---|---|
| May have no legal political parties, or only one | Only one legal political party (Communist Party) | Multiple legal political parties limited electoral freedom |
| Limited or no electoral freedom; rule by a single individual; monarchy may be hereditary or elective | No free elections; rule by a single individual or small group | Rule by people through election although individual or small group may dominate politics |
| Opposition and dissent may be limited or forbidden | Opposition and dissent are limited or forbidden | Opposition and dissent may limited |
| Limited property rights, usually inherited; monarch may claim ownership of entire kingdom | No private property | Limited property rights |
| Government may have significant role in economy | State-controlled economy | Government has significant role in economy |
| Monarch may determine how people are to be employed; forced labor may be required | Officially no unemployment | Unemployment determined b combination of the free marke and government policy |
| Religious freedom may be allowed if it does not threaten the regime, or not, depending on ruler | No freedom of religion | May have religious freedom |
| Social welfare programs may be limited | Limited or no civil liberties or civil rights; widespread social welfare programs (such as free education and health care | Civil liberties and civil rights may be curtailed by government, especially economic rights; widespread social welfare programs (such as free education, health care, and housing) |

| DEMOCRACY | DICTATORSHIP | THEOCRACY |
|---|---|---|
| Multiple legal political parties | Often only one legal political party | Often only one legal political party |
| Free rule by the people through elections | Limited or no electoral freedom; rule by a single individual | Limited or no electoral freedom; rule by a single individual or small group |
| Opposition and dissent are accepted and may be encouraged | Opposition and dissent are limited or forbidden | Opposition and dissent are limited or forbidden |
| Private property protected by law and constitution | Limited property rights | Limited property rights |
| Economy determined by free market | Government may have significant role in economy | Government may have significant role in economy |
| Unemployment determined mainly by the free market | Unemployment determined by combination of the free market and government policy | Unemployment determined by the free market and government policy |
| Freedom of religion | Some religious freedom, if it does not threaten the regime | Religious worship limited to the state religion |
| Widespread and comprehensive civil liberties and civil rights; some social welfare | Limited or no civil liberties and civil rights; social welfare programs are limited | Limited or no civil liberties or civil rights; social welfare programs are limited |

'Monarchy here refers to absolute monarchy, the traditional form of monarchy known in many earlier kingdoms but rare today; modern constitutional monarchies are monarchies in name only and are typically governed as democratic or socialist republics.

# Timeline

**ca. 2300 BCE**
King Naram-Sin of Akkad in Mesopotamia calls himself a god

**ca. 330 BCE**
Aristotle writes *Politics*

**221 BCE**
China is united under the first emperor

**395 CE**
Roman empire is divided into eastern (Constantinople) and western (Rome) empires

**800**
Pope Leo III crowns French ruler Charlemagne emperor

**1215**
King John I of England signs the Magna Carta, accepting limits to royal rule

**1453**
Constantinople falls to Turks

**1600s**
Absolute monarchy emerges in Europe

**1642–1646**
Parliamentarians overthrow monarchy in English Civil War

**1661**
Monarchy is restored in England with coronation of King Charles II

**1688**
In England, Glorious Revolution limits monarchic power and guarantees civil rights

**1776**
Thomas Paine publishes *Common Sense*; American colonies begin revolt from British rule

**1783**
United States constitution establishes new government as democratic republic

**1789**
French Revolution overthrows the French monarchy

**1815**
Congress of Vienna restores traditional dynastic rule to France and other European countries after the Napoleonic Wars

**1867**
Emperor Mutsushito reclaims some imperial authority in Japan and launches the Meiji Era of modernization and reform

**1912**
Chinese empire ends

**1917**
Russian empire falls in communist revolution

**1918**

World War I brings the end of the Austrian and German empires

**1922**

The Ottoman sultanate is abolished in Turkey

**1953**

Queen Elizabeth II of England is crowned, succeeding her father, King George VI

# Nations with Monarchies (2006)

Andorra
Antigua and Barbuda (British Commonwealth)
Australia (British Commonwealth)
Bahamas (British Commonwealth)
Bahrain
Barbados (British Commonwealth)
Belgium
Belize (British Commonwealth)
Bhutan
Brunei
Cambodia
Canada (British Commonwealth)
Denmark
Grenada (British Commonwealth)
Holy See (Vatican City)

# Nations with Monarchies (2006)

Jamaica (British Commonwealth)
Japan
Jordan
Kuwait
Lesotho
Liechtenstein
Luxembourg
Malaysia
Monaco
Morocco
Nepal
Netherlands
New Zealand (British Commonwealth)
Norway
Oman
Papua New Guinea (British Commonwealth)
Qatar
St. Kitts and Nevis (British Commonwealth)
St. Lucia (British Commonwealth)
St. Vincent and the Grenadines (British
  Commonwealth)
Saudi Arabia

Solomon Islands (British Commonwealth)
Spain
Swaziland
Sweden
Thailand
Tonga
Tuvalu (British Commonwealth)
United Arab Emirates
United Kingdom (British Commonwealth)

# Notes

## Chapter 1

p. 10, par. 1, Harold Nicolson, *Monarchy*, London: Weidenfeld and Nicolson, 1962, p. 320.

p. 10, par. 3, www.bbc.co.uk/2536619.st.htm

p. 11, par. 2, Nicolson, *Monarchy*, p. 321.

p. 15, par. 2, Nicolson, *Monarchy*, p. 323.

p. 15, par. 3, Nicolson, *Monarchy*, p. 323.

p. 15, par. 5, Nicolson, *Monarchy*, p. 325.

p. 16, par. 2, Nicolson, *Monarchy*, p. 305.

p. 17, par. 4, Thomas Paine, *Common Sense*, 1776, www.bartleby.com/133/1.html

p. 19, par. 1, Paine, *Common Sense,* www.bartleby.com/133/2.html

p. 19, par. 2, Ibid.

p. 19, par. 3, Ibid.

p. 19, par. 3, Ibid.

p. 21, par. 2, www.mori.com/polls/2000/notw001215.shtml

p. 21, par. 3, www.readersdigest.co.uk.willspoll.htm

p. 21, par. 3, www.mori.com/polls/2004/britishrepublic.shtml

## Chapter 2

p. 23, par. 5, W. M. Spellman, *Monarchies: 1000–2000,* London: Reaktion Books, 2001, p. 12.

p. 23, par. 4, J. N. Postgate, "Royal Ideology and State Administration in Sumer and Akkad," in Jack M. Sasson, ed., *Civilizations of the Ancient Near East,* Vol. 1, New York: Scribner's, 1995.

p. 24, par. 1, Gary Beckman, "Royal Ideology and State Administration in Hittite Anatolia," Sasson, Ibid., p. 530.

p. 26, par. 1, 1 Samuel 8:1–9, *Jerusalem Bible,* Garden City, NY: Doubleday, 1966, p. 302.

p. 31, par. 3, Aristotle, *Politics,* Book III, quoted on the Stanford Encyclopedia of Philosophy website, http://plato.stanford.edu/entries/aristotle-politics/#PolView.html

## Chapter 3

p. 37, par. 1, W. M. Spellman, *Monarchies: 1000–2000,* London: Reaktion Books, 2001, p. 11.

p. 37, par. 3, John King Fairbank, *China: A New History,* Cambridge, MA: Harvard University Press, 1992, p. xvi.

p. 39, par. 1, Spellman, p. 25.

p. 40, par. 5, Spellman, p. 34.

p. 42, par. 1, W. J. F. Jenner, *The Tyranny of History: The Roots of China's Crisis,* London: Harmondsworth, 1992, p. 49.

p. 44, par. 4, Spellman, p. 113.

p. 51, par. 2, Spellman, pp. 142–143.

p. 54, par. 2, Spellman, p. 75.

p. 56, par. 2, Quoted without attribution in Antonia Fraser, *The Warrior Queens,* New York: Vintage Books, 1990, p. 239.

## Chapter 4

p. 70, par. 1, W. M. Spellman, *Monarchies: 1000–2000,* London: Reaktion Books, 2001, p. 152.

p. 71, par. 2, John of Paris, cited in Spellman, p. 186.

p. 71, par. 4, Paolo Prodi, *The Papal Prince,* Cambridge, UK: Cambridge University Press, 1987, p. 17.

p. 75, par. 3, Barbara Hanawalt, *The Middle Ages: An Illustrated History,* New York: Oxford University Press, 1998, pp. 103–104.

## Chapter 5

p. 84, par. 3, Thomas James Dandelet, *Spanish Rome, 1500–1700,* New Haven, CT: Yale University Press, 2001, p. 8.

p. 95, par. 3, Paul Kleber Monod, *The Power of Kings: Monarchy and Religion in Europe, 1589–1715,* New Haven, CT: Yale University Press, 1999, p. 40.

p. 95, par. 4, *Act 24 Henry VIII, xii,* cited in the *Oxford English Dictionary,* Oxford, UK: Oxford University Press, 1971, Micrographic Edition, Volume 1, p. 241.

## Chapter 6

p. 96, par. 1, R. F. Tapsell, *Monarchs, Rulers, Dynasties and Kingdoms of the World,* New York: Facts On File, 1983, p. 11.

p. 96, par. 2, W. M. Spellman, *Monarchies: 1000-2000,* London: Reaktion, 2001, p. 227.

p. 99, par. 2, Spellman, p. 240.

p. 100, par. 1, John Whitney Hall, "A Monarch for Modern Japan," in Robert E. Ward, ed., *Political Development in Modern Japan,* Princeton, NJ: Princeton University Press, 1968, p. 21.

p. 103, par. 1, Binaj Gurubacharya, "Nepalese forces fire again on protestors," *Oregonian,* April 23, 2006, p. A16.

p. 103, par. 4, "Himalayan Horrors," *The Economist,* 375, no. 8422, April 16, 2005, pp. 21–23, www.epnet.com.

p. 103, par. 5 Eirik Helleve, "A Fairytale's Ending," *The World & I,* September 2001, Volume 16, Issue 9, p. 190.

# Further Information

The books and Web sites listed below contain information about monarchy as a system of government or about specific monarchies and dynasties. Some of the books were written especially for young adult readers; the others will not be too difficult for most readers. The Web site addresses were accurate when this book was written, but remember that Web sites and their addresses change frequently. Your librarian can help you find additional resources.

## Books

Blumberg, Arnold, ed. *Great Leaders, Great Tyrants? Contemporary Views of World Leaders Who Made History*. Westport, CT: Greenwood Press, 1995.

Davis, Kenneth C. *Don't Know Much about the Kings and Queens of England*. New York: HarperCollins, 2002.

Hindley, Geoffrey. *The Royal Families of Europe*. New York: Carroll and Graf, 2000.

Lewis, Brenda L. *Monarchy: The History of an Idea*. Stroud, UK: Sutton Books, 2003.

Meltzer, Milton. *Ten Kings and the Worlds They Ruled*. New York: Orchard Books, 2002.

Nicolson, Harold. *Monarchy*. London: Weidenfeld and Nicolson, 1962.

Plain, Nancy. *Louis XVI, Marie-Antoinette, and the French Revolution*. New York: Benchmark Books, 2002.

Schiel, Katy. *Monarchy*. New York: Rosen Publishing Group, 2004.

Tames, Richard. *Monarchy*. London: Heinemann, 2002.

Tapsell, R. F. *Monarchs, Rulers, Dynasties, and Kingdoms of the World*. New York: Facts On File, 1983.

## Web Sites

http://www.classics.mit.edu/index.html
This Massachusetts Institute of Technology site presents the full texts of classic writings, including ancient texts on political theory, such as Plato's *The Republic* and Aristotle's *Politics*.

http://www.eurohistory.com
Maintained by the publisher of the *European Royal History Journal*, this site contains biographical information about European royalty, as well as information on the role of monarchs in politics over the past two centuries.

http://www.guide2womenleaders.com/queens-and-empresses.html
As part of a Web site devoted to women leaders, this page focuses on women who have reigned in their own right or as regents since 1900.

http://www.monarchy.net
The home page of the Constitutional Monarchy Association and the International Monarchist League promotes the view that monarchy has played, and can still play, a positive role. It features quotes by and about monarchs, as well as a reading list and links.

http://www.pwhce.org/monarchylinks.html
The monarchy section of the Perspectives on World History and Current Events site has articles for monarchists as well as links to many sites, including the official Web sites of many of the world's royal families.

http://www.royalty.nu
A collection of links to many sites with information about royalty worldwide, past and present; also offers a reading list and a roundup of recent royal news.

# Bibliography

Ashdown, Dulcie M. *Royal Murders*. Stroud, UK: Sutton, 1998.

Bendix, Reinhard. *Kings or People? Power and the Mandate to Rule*. Berkeley: University of California Press, 1979.

Cannon, John. *The Oxford Illustrated History of the British Monarchy*. New York: Oxford University Press, 2000.

Fraser, Antonia. *The Warrior Queens*. New York: Vintage Books, 1990.

Middleton, John. *Monarchies and Dynasties*. Armonk, NY: M. E. Sharpe, 2005.

Monod, Paul K. *The Power of Kings: Monarchy and Religion in Europe, 1589–1715*. New Haven, CT: Yale University Press, 1999.

Morris, Colin. *The Papal Monarchy*. Oxford, England: Oxford University Press, 1989.

Nenner, Howard. *The Right to Be King*. Chapel Hill: University of North Carolina Press, 1995.

Okey, Robin. *The Habsburg Monarchy: From Enlightenment to Eclipse*. New York: St. Martin's Press, 2001.

Packard, Jerrold M. *Sons of Heaven: A Portrait of the Japanese Monarchy.* New York: Scribner's, 1987.

Roberts, J. M. *History of the World.* Oxford, England: Oxford University Press, 1993.

Spellman, W. M. *Monarchies: 1000–2000.* London: Reaktion Books, 2001.

# Index

Page numbers in **boldface** are illustrations, tables, and charts.

# About the Author

Rebecca Stefoff is the author of many nonfiction books for young adults, including the ten-volume series North American Historical Atlases and the five-volume series World Historical Atlases, and *Marriage,* in our Open for Debate series, all published by Benchmark Books. In addition to books on history, exploration, nature, and science, she has authored works on social history, writing about such topics as environmental activism and legislation, immigration, and Native American rights. Stefoff makes her home in Portland, Oregon. Information about her books for young people can be found at www.rebeccastefoff.com.